Americ
in Woi

MW01193580

ALSO BY HARRY SPILLER AND FROM McFARLAND

Pearl Harbor Survivors: An Oral History of 24 Servicemen (2002)

American POWs in Korea: Sixteen Personal Accounts (1998)

Prisoners of Nazis: Accounts by American POWs
in World War II (1998)

Scars of Vietnam: Personal Accounts by Veterans
and Their Families (1994)

Death Angel: A Vietnam Memoir of a Bearer of
Death Messages to Families (1992)

American POWs in World War II

Twelve Personal Accounts of Captivity by Germany and Japan

HARRY SPILLER

McFarland & Company, Inc., Publishers

Jefferson, North Carolina, and London

LIBRARY OF CONGRESS CATALOGUING-IN-PUBLICATION DATA

Spiller, Harry, 1945–
    American POWs in World War II : twelve personal accounts
of captivity by Germany and Japan / Harry Spiller.
        p.   cm.
    Includes index.

    ISBN 978-0-7864-4275-1
    softcover : 50# alkaline paper ∞

    1. Prisoners of war — United States — Biography.
2. Prisoners of war — Germany — Biography.   3. Prisoners of
war — Japan — Biography.   4. World War, 1939–1945 — Prisoners
and prisons, German.   5. World War, 1939–1945 — Prisoners and
prisons, Japanese.   6. World War, 1939–1945 — Personal narratives,
American.   I. Title.
D805.G3S727   2009
940.54'72092273 — dc22   2009004482

British Library cataloguing data are available

©2009 Harry Spiller. All rights reserved

*No part of this book may be reproduced or transmitted in any form
or by any means, electronic or mechanical, including photocopying
or recording, or by any information storage and retrieval system,
without permission in writing from the publisher.*

On the cover: Near end of death march in Philippines, 1942, Library
of Congress, Prints & Photographs Division, NYWT&S Collection,
LC-USZ62-128769; background ©2008 Shutterstock

Manufactured in the United States of America

*McFarland & Company, Inc., Publishers
    Box 611, Jefferson, North Carolina 28640
    www.mcfarlandpub.com*

To all the ex-prisoners
of World War II
and their families

ACKNOWLEDGMENTS

I would like to thank the former POWs for
sharing their experiences during World War II.
I would also like to give a special thanks to Candice Lahr,
independent book store owner of Cata's Books,
for her editorial assistance
and consulting expertise.

CONTENTS

INTRODUCTION

In World War II, 130,201 American servicemen were captured and held as prisoners of war (POWs). About 25 percent of them were held by the Japanese Imperial Army and the remaining 75 percent were held by Hitler's Third Reich. Although all of these men were POWs in World War II, there were marked differences in the captives' experiences.

The day after the attack on Pearl Harbor, the Japanese began a massive invasion of the West Pacific area. This included Wake Island, the Philippine Islands, Singapore, Southeast Asia, Java, New Guinea, Borneo, and Malaya. By May 1942, after many bloody battles with Allied forces, the Japanese had successfully seized most of the West Pacific. It was during this early part of the war that the Japanese captured the majority of American POWs. These American captives would be prisoners under the Imperial Japanese Army for the entire war.

The Japanese, who believed in fighting to the death, were surprised by the surrender of the Allied Forces in the West Pacific. The surrender posed an unexpected problem for the Japanese: what to do with thousands of Allied prisoners? It also posed a problem for Allied prisoners because, as the Japanese considered surrender unacceptable under any circumstances, they considered POWs inferior beings. This resulted in a cold blooded plan on the part of the Japanese of brutality and extermination.

American prisoners were held in camps scattered in the West Pacific Asia area. Many of the camps were military installations that had been seized by the Japanese during the war. However, in some areas barracks were constructed. Often the barracks had dirt floors. Men slept on the floor, in wooden bunks, or bamboo slabs in the barracks. A latrine was provided, a common open pit with no drainage and filled with maggots and flies.

The Japanese did not adhere to the Geneva Convention at all. Their treatment of American prisoners was barbaric to say the least. Men were bayoneted, tortured, and murdered. On the Bataan Death March alone, 650 American prisoners of war were murdered.

Those lucky enough to survive the inhumane treatment of the Imperial Army were rewarded with hard labor, starvation and disease. Men were forced to work 12 hour days in all weather conditions with only small portions of buggy rice to eat. The food was not enough for the prisoners to maintain their health and many developed diseases from the diet as well as the unsanitary conditions. Due to the lack of medical treatment, many died. Nothing illustrates this better than the construction of the railway in Burma and Thailand. The Japanese needed a supply line to their troops in India and put approximately 300,000 POWs and coolies to work in the most diseased jungles and mountains of Asia. Fifteen months of unspeakable working conditions and treatment killed over half of those men. The railroad was to become known to the world as the Railway of Death.

During the course of the war many of the POWs were moved to various parts of Asia; towards the end of the war large numbers were moved to Japan. One transportation method was the Hell Ships, so named because men in large numbers were stuffed in holes below deck for days and even weeks. There was no ventilation and many suffocated. The dead were thrown overboard, leaving a trail of dead bodies in the Pacific.

When the war was finally over, 12,526 prisoners held by the Japanese never came out of the camps alive, almost 40 percent of the total.

On the other side of the globe Nazi Germany held the other seventy-five percent of American prisoners. The Nazis called them *Kriegsgefangen*— a term that the prisoners of war shortened to *Kriegie*. The nickname became the reality of daily life for a POW.

The first American imprisoned by the Nazis was Navy Lieutenant John Dunn, who was captured on April 14, 1942. On September 25, 1942, the first American Army land troops were reported as prisoners of war by the Nazis to an agency created by the Geneva Convention — the Central Agency for Prisoners of War. From that point until the end of the war Hitler's Third Reich captured a total of 98,312 Americans.

There were three principal types of Nazi prisoner of war camps: the officer Lager (officers' camps), a Stalag Stamm Lager (main camp), and Durchgangs Lager (entrance camp). Seventy-five of these camps were scattered throughout Germany, with a few located in Poland, Czechoslovakia, Austria, and East Prussia. In addition, a number of the prisoners were in Kommandos (work camps) and hospitals.

Most camps had barracks each with a tin roof and a center hallway that ran lengthwise. The rooms were supplied with triple-deck bunk beds with paper sacks filled with straw or wood shavings as mattresses for the prisoners. The washrooms and a pit latrine were located near the rear of the barracks. As the war progressed, many men had to sleep on the floor in the rooms and it became necessary to use the wash rooms to house the prisoners. There were small stoves, tables, and a few stools for furnishings.

The Nazis' adherence to the Geneva Convention was generally correct, but the treatment of American prisoners of war by the Third Reich depended largely on the prisoner's location, the time period in which the prisoner was captured, and what German units were in charge of the prisoners — regular German army or SS troops.

For example, Stalag Luft III proved to be a well organized camp of captured Air Force officers with some of the best treatment as compared to other prison camps, while Stalag VII was a camp of captured enlisted ground forces with average treatment as compared to other prison camps, and Stalag IXB, established for enlisted men captured during the Von Rundstedt Offensive of December 1944, gave poor treatment to prisoners.

Throughout the war, the deterioration of the German transportation system impaired proper segregation of prisoners according to nationalities and removal of prisoners from the danger of air raids. Food, clothing, and medical supplies were severely rationed among the Germans and were scarce for the prisoners of war. There is no doubt that the Nazis made numerous willful violations of the convention ranging from technicalities to full-scale atrocities.

Another factor affecting the treatment of prisoners was the attitude of the German soldiers themselves. There was a sharp division between the attitudes of the German regular army and Adolf Hitler's SS troops toward the POWs. The regular army willfully violated many rules — holding back Red Cross packages and clothing, claiming that there were shortages of food and water as a result of bombing raids, making threats of beatings and death, and ignoring medical needs of prisoners, to name a few. There were atrocities by the regular army — beatings, prisoners killed, terrorizing by police dogs, and placement in solitary confinement to name a few — but atrocities by the regular army were more of an exception than a rule.

The SS (*Schutzstaffel* or Protective Squadron) troops were a different story. Their attitude toward prisoners and human life was so grossly twisted that many of the regular army troops feared them. American prisoners were beaten, tortured and murdered by the SS troops. Some were beaten and murdered upon capture, others while they were in prison camp, and some after attempting to escape. Records from the Nuremburg trials show that at the death camps — Flossenburg Concentration Camp and Mauthasen Concentration Camp — American prisoners were killed by the SS troops. Fifteen members of an American mission in Slovakia were executed. Over six hundred American prisoners of war were found in the Buchenwald and Dachau Gestapo concentration camps at the end of the war.

The Germans surrendered three months before the Japanese. When the war ended, slightly more than 1000 American prisoners, 1.1 percent of the total number, had died in Nazi camps.

To get a true picture of what life was like for a prisoner of war — to be beaten, threatened with death, to ache with hunger, to watch helplessly as your friends died from diseases common among prisoners such as tuberculosis, ulcers, gastritis, nephritis, dysentery, and diarrhea, to face the unknown of what each day might bring — one needs to walk in the footsteps of the men who lived as prisoners of war.

This book contains 12 personal accounts of men who fought the Japanese and Nazis only to face the grim reality of daily life as prisoners of war. The stories run the gamut from Wake Island, the Death Railway, the Bataan Death March, and survival in the jungles of Burma after escaping the Japanese, to the D-Day invasion, B-17 crew members shot down over Germany and the Battle of the Bulge.

I was born in 1945 just before the end of the war and grew up hearing stories and watching movies about World War II. This era has continued to fascinate me and is the inspiration for writing this book. The information for the book came from personal interviews with ex-prisoners of war, personal documents of ex-prisoners of war, military records from the National Archives in Washington D.C., the U.S. Navy Department in Washington, D.C., and the National Headquarters of American Ex-prisoners of War, the Provost Marshal's Office of the U.S. Army, American Red Cross documents, and the War Department in Washington, D.C.

The stories in this book are real, they are compelling, and they give a true picture of men's lives as American prisoners in World War II.

— 1 —

GUNNERY SERGEANT EDWARD STURGEON U.S. MARINE CORPS

1st Defense Battalion, 5th Artillery Wake Island
Captured While in Defense of Wake Island
Prisoner of War
December 23, 1941–September 6, 1945
Woosung, China, and Osaka, Japan

The Beginning: June 11, 1941–November 2, 1941

On June 11, 1941, 19-year-old Edward Sturgeon joined the Marine Corps and was sent to the Marine Corps Recruit Depot in San Diego, California, for boot camp. The Japanese aggression in the Pacific had gotten so bad at the time, boot camp had been shortened by a month. After eight weeks of rigorous training, Ed graduated from boot camp and was assigned to the 8th Marines in San Diego.

One day at roll call the platoon sergeant asked for volunteers for the 1st Defense Battalion in Hawaii. Those who volunteered would get out of all the day to day training. Ed volunteered. For the next two weeks, the volunteers spent fifteen minutes doing close order drill in the morning and the rest of the day at the Slop Shute drinking beer.

In September 1941, Ed and the other volunteers loaded aboard a ship. A week later they arrived in Hawaii and were transported to the 1st Defense Barracks located at Pearl Harbor. For the next couple of weeks Ed and the other men stayed busy with infantry training and close order drill.

The first week of October, the 1st Defense unit received orders that they were restricted to the base. Ed knew they were going to be shipped out, but information was so secret at the time they didn't know when or where.

A week later, the 1st Defense Battalion boarded ship and headed west. They traveled in a complete blackout with two destroyer escorts. Ed and the rest of the crew took turns day and night standing submarine watch in case of an attack by the Japanese. A few days later they arrived at Johnson Island without incident. After dropping off some supplies, they headed out again.

This time it wasn't the Japanese they were concerned about. It was the weather. They had headed straight into a typhoon. As Ed recalled, "You could look over the side of the ship and the waves were so high that you couldn't see the destroyers. We had to eat sandwiches and drink coffee for about three days. When you were at a table you didn't know whose coffee you were drinking, you just had to grab a cup as it came by. I decided I wasn't going to get sick, but I saw all these other guys vomiting and it made me seasick. Finally, the weather cleared up and we could go above deck. To my surprise we were circling an island. The ship had to anchor out about a quarter of a mile because there were no channels to bring the ships in to dock. We had arrived at Wake Island."

A Brief History

Wake Island is one of the most isolated islands in the world inhabited by people. It sits in the center of the Pacific with map coordinates of 19 16' N., 166 37' E. The islands are 2,000 miles west of Hawaii, 1,200 miles east of Guam, and 1,000 miles southwest of Midway Islands.

Three islands make up the V shaped land mass. The largest is named Wake and is located at the point of the V. At each end of the arms of Wake Island's V are two small islands that are less than a mile long. Peale Island is the northern island and Wilkes Island is on the south side. An ancient volcano and lagoon are cradled by the three islands. A coral reef almost encompasses the nine mile outer perimeter.

The first known sighting of Wake Island occurred in 1586 by Spanish explorer Alvaro de Mendana. In his brief stay looking for supplies of food and water, he discovered the only inhabitants to be birds and rats that could stand on their hind legs. In 1796 a British merchant by the name

Aerial view of Wake Island, taken one month after the prisoners were moved to Japan (National Archives, Washington, D.C.).

of Samuel Wake visited the island. Forty-four years later in 1840 Commodore Charles Wilkes, a U.S. Naval officer, and naturalist Titian Peale surveyed the island. Named for these three men — Wake, Wilkes, and Peale — collectively the islands became known as Wake Island.

The island remained uninhabited until Pan American Airways established a station there for refueling its trans–Pacific Clippers in the mid 1930s. By the time Edward Sturgeon arrived on November 2, 1941, Wake had become a military base. He and his fellow volunteers brought the force on the island to 15 officers, 373 enlisted men, a Navy doctor and one hospital corpsman.

The First Days on Wake: November 2, 1941–December 7, 1941

Upon arrival at Wake Island on November 2, 1941, Edward Sturgeon and the other Marines were assigned to living quarters and given duty assignments. Here is Ed's personal account.

9

"The first thing that I noticed about the island was how white the coral was. It actually hurt my eyes for a while until I got used to it. We were assigned to four-men tents. We had hard cots to sleep on and had to take salt water showers. After the shower, I was walking back to the tent and I noticed there were rats all over the place. They went about their business as if none of us were around. I did the same. I put my gear away and hit the bunk. About 2:00 A.M. the next morning they came down the line and wanted a volunteer mess cook. I volunteered for the job.

"I went to the kitchen, which was just another tent with screen sides built onto it. All we had to cook with was wood. The civilian contractors would dump wood and I would get up each morning about 4:00 A.M., cut up wood and get the stoves fired up. The one day that I remember most is Thanksgiving Day. We were supposed to have turkey, but when we got the supply of turkey they were all spoiled. Instead we had ox tongue and rice.

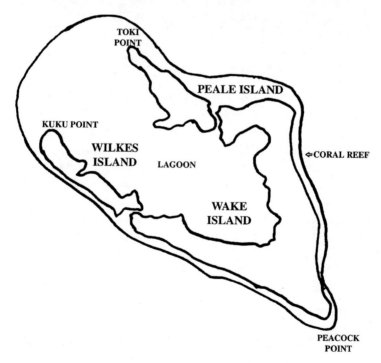

Map of Wake Island (drawn by Harry Spiller).

"I kept busy for about thirty days firing up the stoves, but December 7, that ended. I lost my job when new diesel burning stoves arrived for the kitchen."

The Battle of Wake Island: December 8, 1941–December 23, 1941

The next morning, on December 8, having been temporarily replaced by diesel burning stoves, Ed was milling around the tent. A fellow bunk mate darted through the door. "The Japs attacked Pearl Harbor," he yelled out. The two Marines locked eyes and stood silently glaring at each other in awe.

In a short time the entire 1st Defense Battalion had received the news. The United States was at war with the Japanese. Four planes were put in the air immediately. They flew at 12,000 feet with men watching for any signs of an attack by the Japanese. In the meantime Ed had gone to the mess hall for chow, as he recounted, "We were in the mess hall and the air raid alarms went off. We ran out and got in trucks and headed for our gun positions. I was on a 5-inch gun at Toki Point and was there in minutes. We only had 12 planes on Wake Island that had arrived about a week before the war started. The bomb racks didn't fit and had to be reworked. We still put four in the air to look for Japanese. A little after 1200 noon 36 Jap bombers came in on us. Our planes couldn't spot them because they came in real low in a V formation and cut their engines just before coming over the island. We didn't know they were there until they were right on top of us and then all hell broke loose. They did a lot of damage. All of our planes except four in the air were destroyed. Some of the men in the air squadron were killed as well as several civilians. They did a lot of damage to Camp One and Two and destroyed a lot of our storage tanks. Some of our anti-aircraft guns fired back, but we didn't hit a plane."

The next morning before daylight on December 9 the general quarters alarm sounded again. Ed and the rest of the gun crew watched in the early morning darkness for signs of the Japanese. It wasn't until about noon when they hit with a bombing raid again. The Marines stayed in position and this time they were ready for the attack. The anti-craft guns shot into the Japanese tight V-formations with deadly accuracy. By the time the planes left, six were trailing smoke and one of those disintegrated in the air.

The Japanese were not without some success, however. They had rained 500 pound bombs on the island and a number of buildings were destroyed. As Ed explained, "We were lucky because one of the apparent targets was the 3-inch guns at Battery E and the 5-inch guns at Battery A located at Peacock Point. These positions guarded the southern approach to the island and the positions received some damage. We weren't hit."

On the third day, December 10, the defenders were weary from the lack of sleep and the daily bombing. They were also well dug in. An American F4F-3 Wildcat fighter plane intercepted the Japanese before they arrived at the island on this third attack and shot two planes down. The Japanese arrived early for their attack on Wake with 25 planes at about 10:45 A.M. Obviously, they were concentrating on the gun positions with this attack. This time, Edward recalled, his crew wasn't so lucky. "One of the first targets was our guns. They did some damage this time, knocking out the aiming scope on one gun, and they destroyed some of the ammo. One thing paid off though. The night before, we moved some of our 3 inch guns and we had constructed some wooden dummy guns. They destroyed the dummies, but didn't touch any of the 3 inch guns."

On December 11, at about three in the morning, the defenders spotted the invasion force. Edward explained, "That night we knew they were going to try an invasion. They wanted to sneak in on us, but the sea was too rough for a landing. We found out later that there were several of their men killed as they tried to load aboard landing craft. At daylight, they came in with 13 ships. They started shelling us and artillery rounds were hitting all around us. We held our fire. They came in a little closer and continued firing while we waited. As the ships got closer we could see that they had three cruisers, six destroyers, and four transport ships. Finally they came in within 500 yards and we got orders to open fire. The first shot we fired, all you could see was feathers. The recoil blew our bedding all to hell. I'll never forget that. We had them in a trap. We hit eight ships and sank two destroyers before they could pull out. We stopped their land invasion and it was the first time in the war that an invasion by the Japs had been stopped."

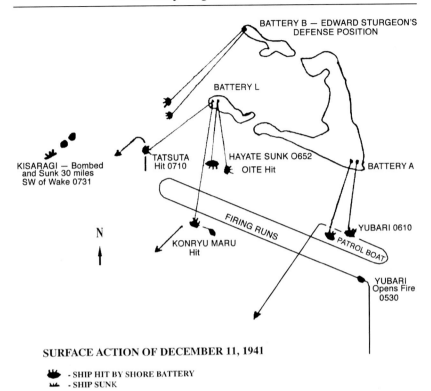

BATTERY B — EDWARD STURGEON'S DEFENSE POSITION

BATTERY L

HAYATE SUNK 0652

OITE Hit

TATSUTA Hit 0710

KISARAGI — Bombed and Sunk 30 miles SW of Wake 0731

BATTERY A

N

FIRING RUNS

KONRYU MARU Hit

YUBARI 0610

PATROL BOAT

YUBARI Opens Fire 0530

SURFACE ACTION OF DECEMBER 11, 1941

- SHIP HIT BY SHORE BATTERY
- SHIP SUNK

Surface action of December 11, 1941 (drawn by Harry Spiller).

Ed and the other defenders' spirits were high with their victory over the overwhelming odds of the Japanese attack. They spent most of the night moving guns and by morning they were ready to rest. The Japanese, however, planned to continue the pressure on the defenders. They attacked at 5:00 A.M., strafing the gun positions and the airfield.

On the fifth day another first came for the defenders when one of the Wildcat pilots spotted a submarine off the shores of Wake. The pilot attacked and made a direct hit on the Japanese submarine, which in minutes left only an oil slick on the surface of the ocean. For the next ten days the defenders fell into a routine. The daily bombings were clockwork. The days became indistinguishable as the men dealt with attending to their wounded, burying their dead, and preparing for the next raid.

Life in the foxholes was anything but pleasant. Rats were running everywhere. Often when the men tried to get a few minutes of sleep they would be awakened by rats running across their bodies. Dead birds were everywhere. In between bombings, efforts were made to get food to the defenders, but often food consisted of cranberries or orange marmalade out of a can for some, while many went for several days without food at all.

Then on December 23, after ten days of constant bombing, the Japanese made the final assault. More than 1,000 soldiers with the essential equipment boarded landing craft and landed at approximately 1:00 A.M. The battle for Wake was on. The outnumbered defenders fought savagely against overwhelming odds. Finally, after seven hours of battle, the decision was made to surrender. At 8:00 A.M. the command began to alert all units by telephone to cease fire. The battle for Wake Island was over.

Prisoners on Wake:
December 23, 1941–January 12, 1942

The Japanese were in complete control on the island and began to collect the American prisoners. Ed recalled the events of capture and the days to follow: "After we surrendered we waited at the gun sight for them to come after us. We slept as much as we could because we hadn't had any sleep for days. It was about noon when they got us. They were jabbering all the time. All they wanted was money. They were running around, 'money, money, money.' Every once in a while they would find a 10 or 20 dollar bill and they would just throw it in the air. They didn't want that, they wanted silver. 'Watch, watch,' they jabbered.

"They made us strip so they could search us good then they let us put our clothes back on. We were lucky, though, because we were the last of the prisoners picked up. The first prisoners they captured were stripped and had their hands tied behind them with telephone wire, which then ran up around their necks. Then they started beating them.

"They took us to the airfield and made us sit there in the open field. The sun was hot and they wouldn't give us any water. The people that were injured had gotten no treatment and they were starting to smell from the infection in their wounds. That first night it rained and the wind began to blow. Some of the guys didn't have any shirts and even for those of us who did, it got really cold.

"The second day, we were crowded together. The Japanese came out with machine guns and set them up all around us. They were just getting ready to pull the trigger when it started raining again, so they covered their machine guns up. It rained for an hour or so. When it quit raining the Japanese came back out and uncovered their guns. They were going to shoot us, and just as they were going to start, a Japanese admiral came up waving his hands and yelling at them to stop. They moved their machine guns and left us there for the rest of the day. Late in the afternoon, they brought us the first food, dried bread. None of us had any water in two days. They used empty gas barrels to carry water to us. The water tasted like gasoline.

"On Christmas day, they took us into a barrack that had not been bombed out. They strung barbed wire around the barracks so we couldn't get out. They had guards all around the fence. It was better to be out of the weather and they gave us some stew that day to eat, but I was still getting really hungry. The day that the war started we had scattered food all over the island and hid it. I knew where I had hidden a case of sardines so I went under the fence that night and went out there and got a few cans of sardines.

"Things were really pleasant in the camp at that time. There were no beatings or anything. They pretty much left us alone. We had destroyed most of the weapons before we were captured, but we hadn't gotten to destroy all of them, so a couple of days later some Jap guards came to the barracks and took six of us to a building to clean the .50-caliber machine guns that they had captured. They stood outside while we worked. We took a part out of every gun.

"Across the road from us they filled one of the barracks full of food. I went over and all the windows were broken out of the barracks, so I climbed in and got some of the Jap crackers. They were like our C-ration crackers and we called them Japanese heart attacks. I liked them better than our crackers because they were sweeter.

"Then in January 1942, they came around and told us to pack we were leaving. We had no idea where we were going."

On January 12, 1942, most of the prisoners were able to travel. All but 20 of the Wake Island prisoners were taken to a ship waiting offshore, the *Nitta Meru*. (The *Nitta Meru* and other Japanese ships used to transport prisoners were named Hell Ships by the prisoners because of the inhumane treatment and conditions they had to endure.) The regulations read as follows:

JAPANESE NAVAL REGULATIONS FOR PRISONERS OF WAR

Commander of the Prisoner Escort
Navy of the Great Japanese Empire

REGULATIONS FOR PRISONERS

1. The prisoners disobeying the following orders will be punished with immediate death:

    a. Those disobeying orders and instructions
    b. Those showing a motion of antagonism and raising a sign of opposition.
    c. Those disordering the regulations by individualism, egoism, thinking only about yourself, rushing for your own goods.
    d. Those talking without permission and raising loud voices.
    e. Those walking and moving without order.
    f. Those carrying unnecessary baggage in embarking.
    g. Those resisting mutually.
    h. Those touching the boat's materials, wires, electric lights, tools, switches, etc.
    i. Those climbing ladder with out order.
    j. Those showing action of running away from the room or boat.
    k. Those trying to take more meal than is giving to them.
    l. Those using more than two blankets.

2. Since the boat is not well equipped and inside being narrow, food being scarce and poor you'll feel uncomfortable during the short time on the boat. Those losing patients and disobeying the regulation will be heavily punished for the reason of not being.

3. Be sure to finish your "Nature Call," evacuate the bowels and urine before embarking.

4. Meals will be given twice a day. One plate only to one prisoner. The prisoners called by the guard will give out the meal quick as possible and honestly. The remaining prisoners will stay in their places quietly and wait for your plate.

5. Toilet will be fixed at the four corners of the room. The buckets and cans will be placed. When filled up a guard will appoint a prisoner.

The prisoner called will take the buckets to the center of the room. The buckets will be pulled up by the derrick and be thrown away. Toiler papers will be given. Everyone must cooperate to make sanitary. Those being careless will be punished.

6. Navy of the Great Japanese Empire will not try to punish you all with death. Those obeying all the rules and regulations, and believing the action and purpose of the Japanese Navy, cooperating with Japan in constructing the "New order of the Great Asia" which lead to the world's peace will be well treated.

The End

During the twelve-day voyage the men endured beatings and starvation, and five of the prisoners were brutally executed. The victims of the horrible atrocity were Seaman First Class John W. Lambert, Seaman Second Class Theodore D. Franklin, Seaman Second Class Roy J. Gonzales, Master Sergeant Earl R. Hannum, and Technical Sergeant William Bailey. All were beheaded and no one knows why or how these five men were chosen for the execution. The ship stopped first in Japan then continued to prison camps in Woosung and Kiangwan, China.

Ed recalled his experience of the twelve-day voyage on the hell ship. "The first part of January they came in and told us to pack some of our clothing that we were leaving. We didn't know where we were going, so we packed the warmest clothing we had. We got our clothing together and they loaded us on a small boat to go out to the ship, which was anchored about a quarter of a mile out. The sea was really rough that day. They had a ladder lowered on the side of the ship and we were trying to climb aboard. Guys were getting knocked off the ladder. Some of them were getting injured. The Japs decided that wouldn't work so they took us around on the other side of the boat and lowered a rope. It looked like it was about twenty feet up. The boat we were in would be next to the ship one minute then rock as far as fifteen away from it the next minute. Each one of us had to grab the rope, swing against the side of the ship with our feet, and walk and pull ourselves up the side. There were sharks in the water so we had to be careful not to slip. All of us remembered the Jap ships we sank and not a single Jap made it to shore because of the sharks. I grabbed the rope and swung over. I was weak from the lack of food, but I thought about the sharks and I was able to muster enough strength to make it to the deck.

"When we got to the top, the whole Jap crew was lined up in two lines. All of them were carrying clubs. The first thing they did was to take all of our clothes that we had brought with us. Then they made us run through the line while they beat us with their clubs. I did better than some, but I was hit in the head several times. It caused a brain abscess which required me to have a brain operation later. That was the first brutal treatment we got.

"Then they put us below deck. We were down there for 12 days. They would come in every so often yelling and screaming at us, then they would beat us with clubs. We got a bucket to use for human waste. They gave us a little bowl of GUI water called soup. We called it slop. Several days out to sea it started to get cold. We didn't have any clothes other than those on our backs and we thought we were going to freeze to death. One day their general quarters sounded off. We heard later from some of the men that they heard two torpedoes go by.

"After approximately one week we pulled up at Tokyo and they took a few prisoners off and then we took off again. When we stopped again we were at the docks at Shanghai, China. The 12 day voyage ended on January 24, 1942. It was spitting snow and sleet and most of the guys had on shorts and summer shirts. None of us had hats or coats. They made us walk about six miles to Woosung. Many of the guys just about froze to death on the march to the prison camp."

Woosung prison camp is located 15 miles north of Shanghai and 5 miles northeast of Woosung Forts. It was originally a Chinese army training camp. It was captured by the Japanese in 1937 and used as a Japanese army barracks. The camp consisted of eight one-story barracks, each approximately 300 feet long by 35 feet wide. The barracks were sectioned on the inside and provided living space for 24 men.

The sleeping decks rose approximately a foot from the floor, and the prisoners sat on them when they ate. Each prisoner was issued one cotton mattress sack with straw filling, a small straw filled pillow, and two cotton filled blankets to fight off the bitter winter. At night the rats scurried through the barracks freely.

The latrine was located at the end of the barracks. It was constructed so the waste discharged into large earthen jars located underneath the floor. Chinese coolies would empty these jars and carry the waste to their fields for fertilizer. Two electric fences were used to control the 1,500 prisoners in the camp. One was located around the eight barracks and the other bordered the entire camp.

Welcome to Woosung: January 24, 1942–September 1942

"They put us in the barracks with no heat," Ed explained. "About midnight they came by and gave us some soup. It had curry powder in it. You talk about warming someone up.

"For the next couple of months they didn't make us do any work. It was a good thing, too, because we were on a starvation diet of about 500 calories a day. We got a small bowl of rice, a bowl of stew, and tea. After a couple of months they increased the diet to about 650 grams of rice plus some meat. It wasn't long before the meat was cut out of the diet. The only supply of water was from a 30 foot well and we were warned not to drink it. All we had was tea. We fed our hogs better, but we had to eat the food because that is all they gave us. Every once in a while we would catch a rat in the barracks and eat it. They didn't taste all that bad.

"After a couple of months they started working us ten hour days. We worked at leveling a field which was used for a Japanese parade ground. Some of the men worked on farms and others on roads. I worked on a farm and road repair. It didn't matter what the weather was, we had to work out in it. Also, the work was hard considering the lack of food. I was suffering from dysentery, malnutrition, and rapid weight loss.

"To add to the misery the guards' treatment got worse as time passed. Face slapping became a common occurrence. Mass punishment occurred on several occasions. If just one prisoner messed up all of us had to pay. They made us stand in the rain for long hours. Sometimes they stopped food for days. All of us were suffering from the conditions and treatment. Then, I got the word that I was being moved."

Osaka Ship Yards:
September 1942–September 1945

The Osaka Prison Camps housed approximately 10,000 POWs. It was run by Colonel Akami. It was rumored that Colonel Akami had served in China, but had gone mad during the battle and was returned to his homeland to do a less stressful job. He was brutal to the prisoners and was executed after the war for his actions.

The barracks at the prison were wooden houses approximately 18 feet wide and 33 feet long and housed approximately 75 men. Water was provided by outside spigots at wooden wash tables. The bunks were made of rough cut lumber and were stacked in threes. They were covered by a thin straw mat. The mat was a little comfort against the rough lumber. The personal belongings of the prisoners were placed on a narrow wooden ledge on the wall just behind the sleeping shelves.

Ed was loaded aboard another hell ship in September 1942 and headed for Japan. The ship held close to the coastal lines, going back in case of a torpedo attack. The captors were more decent to the prisoners this trip. They let prisoners come up on deck about fifteen minutes a day and gave them some food. The prisoners received no beatings. A few days later they arrived in Kobe, Japan. The Japanese transferred the prisoners to a variety of jobs as slave laborers in lumber yards, junk yards, steel mills, cement factories, warehouses, barges, sampans, and coal mines.

Daily life for the prisoners was grueling. The Japanese controlled their every move. They told them when to get up, what they would eat, and where, when, and how long they would work. In return, the captors did little more than provide some of the bare necessities.

Ed was assigned to the shipyards at Osaka. "Several of the men refused to work and they were killed," he explained. "We knew they meant business, so when they said to work, you worked. We worked at hard labor 12 hours a day. There were no safety precautions for us, but I guess we were better off than some because they had to work in the coal mines without any safety precautions. They made us carry big slabs of steel on our backs from one location to another. The slabs we carried averaged 300 pounds. In the summer it was hot, in the winter freezing cold. The Japs issued us one jacket in the winter and we had to work out in the weather regardless of whether it was snowing, sleeting, or raining. We would get soaked in the rain then go back to the barracks with no heat. I was getting weak from the lack of food and I was afraid I wouldn't be able to work. My weight loss had brought me down to less than one hundred pounds. I had dysentery and beri beri. We had no medical care, so if a prisoner couldn't work anymore they were placed in barracks to die. To make it worse, their food rations were cut in half.

"The Japs decided that they were going to train some riveters. I thought this would be a good way to get away from carrying the steel and get out of the weather. I volunteered for the training and in a short time I was working on the ships. I watched the Japs and noticed that they weren't checking my work, so I started putting loose rivets in the overhead of the ship. Then one day they lined us up and I thought they may have found out what we were doing. Instead, they told us how we were great ship builders. They said they never had any ships return for repairs. We joked about it later because we knew why they weren't coming back. It was because they were being sunk by our Navy as fast as they went out.

"This job was easier than packing 300 pound slabs on my back, but I was getting weaker. At that time the rice we got was the sweepings off the floors. The rice was full of rat droppings and rocks. It just wasn't fit to eat. The Japs got a shipment of tangerines in and we were so hungry we would follow them around and pick up their peelings and eat them.

"At the yards they had an old skinny horse. We used to make fun of it all the time. One day it was killed during a bombing raid. It had been hit by incendiary bombs. It was burnt and laying in the mud. The Japs told us we could have the horse to eat. We dragged it out of the mud, cleaned it up, and butchered it. The Japs took the meat and gave us the bones. We actually had every bone in the horse. We ate what we could from the bone and sucked the juice out of the bones.

"We knew if we were caught stealing food they would kill us, but we were starving. Some of the guys were stealing rice and I was stealing rock salt. Some guys had stolen electrical parts and had made homemade hot plates with the parts. They hid them in the walls of the barracks. We used the hot plates and traded what food we stole to stay alive.

"The Japs were getting short on food and we probably would have forgiven them if they had just starved us, but we had to take the beatings too. They beat us all the time. They made excuses for the least little thing.

Every time we would take back an island or something they would beat the hell out of us with a two-inch bamboo club. They would hit us in the head and around the face. Some of the guys got their ears split from the beatings. I never got my ears split, but I did get hit in the head really hard. Then things got worse when we took back Okinawa. They beat us daily. We laughed at them all the time. They would beat us and we would laugh about it later. It used to make them mad because they couldn't break our spirit.

"In 1943, in Osaka, Japan, we had an Army Air Corps sergeant that was a radioman. He worked out around the Jap ships and he stole the parts to make a radio. He got the news from the radio. The Japs found out we had the radio, but they couldn't find it. They started beating everyone to find it. In the meantime he took it apart and threw it in the toilet. After a while he saw that the Japs were beating on everybody else so he told then where it was. They made him go down in the toilet up to his neck in waste and get the parts out. When he came out, he smelled terrible. Then they took him to this cell and put him in it. All he could do was stand in it. He couldn't sit or lay because there wasn't any room. There were sticks sharpened and pointing toward him on all sides so that if he fell or tried to bend they would stick him.

"The second day we noticed that the Japs would take him out of the cell and to the toilet at the same time. So we gathered up food and one of us would be in the toilet because the Japs would wait outside. When he came in, we would feed him. We did that day after day. He was getting more food than we were at the time. The Japs never caught on to what we were doing. They left him there for 12 days just standing there except for the once a day toilet trip. After the 12 days the Japs let him out and went to gibbering and carrying on. They got food and fed him really well. We were surprised until we learned that the Japs thought he was a hero. They couldn't believe that a man could stand for 12 days without food or water."

1945 Bombing Raids Over Japan

Since the Americans had taken Guam and Saipan, American bombers were able to operate within the Japanese homeland. Wave after wave of B-29 bombers dropped tons of bombs on the enemy.

Ed recalled, "The first part of 1945, the B-29's started coming over and we figured the war was getting short. Then in March 1945, 300 B-29's burnt the whole city of Osaka out with incendiary bombs. Some of the bombs landed right in our barracks. Some of the guys got their faces burnt and some got teeth knocked out, but none were killed. We were really happy to see that, even if the bombs were dropped on us. One of the funniest things was the Japs had a fire department right beside our barracks and it burnt down before they could get the fire trucks out of it.

"A few days later they loaded us aboard a train and we headed north through Tokyo and all the way across the island to Aoshi, Japan, to the steel mills. The first thing they did was to cut our food rations. We worked day after day and they just kept cutting our food rations lower and lower because of the shortage of the food supply. We would get up each day and work 12 hour days around those hot furnaces. We were told that during the winter it got as low as 30 below zero so we were lucky from that standpoint.

"Every fifth day we would have to work a 24-hour shift because we would change from day shift to night shift. I was really getting weak. Then the fleas were really getting bad. They were all over me biting. It was terrible. We had to jump up and bow to the Jap soldiers when they came by and I had gotten my temper up over the fleas and the whole mess we were in, so I decided that I wasn't going to bow to them anymore. One of these little Japs came by and I didn't get up. He went to gibbering and grabbed me and took me outside. He started beating me with his club. I decided that I wasn't going to let the little son-of-a-bitch knock me down, but after he beat me for a while he did knock me down. After that he made me stand out there all night long. Every time they changed guards they would beat the hell out of me.

"We knew that the Japs had orders to kill all of us in case the Americans landed in Japan. As a matter of fact, if they hadn't dropped the atom bomb we would have been [killed]. They already had some of the graves dug. We would be working in the factories and we made knives and carried them back to the camp. They would search us. I don't care what you had, as long as you showed it to them, they didn't care. I don't know why, but the only thing that they had a concern about is what you had hid on your body."

The Final Days

"The commander of the camp had several ducks and a big pig that were running around the camp. I guess he was trying to torment us because we were so hungry. We wouldn't bother trying to get any of them, though, because if one person got caught trying to steal food then everyone got punished. They may make us do without food for two or three days or they may make someone go out and stand in the hot sun with their hands in the air until they passed out. One day, about a week after I was beaten, I went out and lined up for work. I was on the night shift. The Japs came out and they were gibbering and carrying on. Then they said, 'Nice Noto, Nice Noto' (no work in Japanese). We got to talking and figured that something was happening. About an hour later the day shift came walking into the camp. The Japs never told us the war was over, but we thought it might be. That night we got up the nerve to sleep outside so that we could get away from the fleas. The next morning when we woke up the Jap guards were gone except for a couple of the good guards. They never said a word to us all day.

"The second day, I got enough nerve and decided that I was going to get a duck. I waited all day and when it got dark, I went out to get one. There weren't any ducks left. The other prisoners had already got them. Well, I went back in and several of us got to talking about the big hog. We didn't know the war was over, but we knew there was a good chance it was so we went over, got the pig and killed it. The Japs didn't say a word. One of the guys looked down at the gate where the Jap guard was. He said he had enough and went down to the gate and took the rifle away from the Jap. We headed to town. Women would be outside with their chickens and ducks. We would just walk up in a yard and grab the biggest chickens and ducks. Then we found a five-gallon can of peanut oil and that night we had the biggest chicken fry you ever saw.

"The next day some of the guys went to town and found a shortwave radio set and found out the war was over. That was the first that we officially knew it was over. That same day an American plane came over and dropped a parachute with magazines and cigarettes. The day following another plane came over and dropped some more. They circled and told us that B-29's would be over the next day to drop food to us. So we were excited and the next morning we got up early. Eighteen B-29's came in and they were low. They opened their bomb bay doors and came in right over the top of us. They released several containers, two 55 gallon drums which were welded together, and the parachutes busted on them. We were out in the yard dodging barrels. Some of the guys got hit by them and were injured. They had done this all over Japan and we heard that a few of the POWs were killed. The barrels were full of fruit and all the things we needed. That night one of the guys got on the shortwave and made contact with the Americans. They told them that we had gotten the food, but if they were going to try to kill us that we might as well stay there. They got the point.

"The next day the planes came in again. They dropped food again. I had dropped from 165 pounds on Wake Island to 89 pounds at the end of the war. It was estimated that we were gaining three pounds a day on the food we were getting. I could certainly stand to gain, we all could. They also dropped clothing. The thing that always sticks in my mind is the shoes. I guess they wanted to make sure that we got the right size because when we left the camp there was a pile of shoes as high as a mountain.

"The morning of September 6, 1945, some of the guys decided that we needed to catch a train and go to Tokyo. We asked one of the Japs to take us and he wasn't going to do it, so one of the Marines pulled a gun on him. Then the Jap took us. We shoveled coal and the Jap engineer drove the train. All the men that died in China were buried, but the men who died in Japan had to be cremated. When we left the prison camp, we brought all of them back with us.

"We went across the island to the American forces in Yokohama. The first thing that I saw was the American uniforms on the 1st Cavalry Army division. It was a wonderful sight. The Red Cross was there and they gave us a candy bar. Then they took us in and deloused us. Then they gave us new clothes and more food."

Heading Home: September 1945–May 1946

"The next morning, September 7, 1945, they took us by boat out in the harbor to the USS *Ozark*. It was late when we got aboard the ship and they were going to feed us. We lined up at the chow line. The Navy thought we hadn't eaten and they didn't want to over feed us. They didn't know we had been getting food dropped to us, so the first thing they did was drop vitamin pills and then sloppy soup. It was just soup, but it was good. It was like they were putting us on a diet. That night we broke into the food lockers and got some good food. The next day they fed us a good meal.

"We pulled out and got into Guam a few days later. I got paid and went to the PX and bought some candy bars. I ate 22 chocolate bars that day. It is a wonder it didn't kill me. They put us in a hospital for a few days. It was funny because you would wake up in the morning and most of the guys would be laying on the floor. We couldn't sleep on the soft mattresses.

"A few days later we sailed and arrived in Hawaii. They let us off at Pearl Harbor and after two days we headed for the States. When we arrived in San Francisco there were newspaper people waiting for us, but we were told that we were not to tell how we were treated in the camps because if we did we would be court-martialed. They took us to the Naval Hospital in Oakland. I stayed there for three or four days.

"Then one morning they loaded us aboard a train headed for Chicago. We had about twenty cars to the train. I don't know how many men we had on the train, but they were all POWs from Corregidor, the Philippines, and Wake. Guys started writing on the side of the train. We took off and after a while the train stopped in a town. All the prisoners got off the train and headed across the street to the local taverns. At the first stop the train was two hours getting started again. As the guys were getting back on the train, you would see one with a case of beer, another with a case of whiskey. We had enough liquor on the train to last six months.

"The train started off and just as it did there was a colored woman walking by the train carrying a bucket. One of the guys grabbed the bucket from her and filled it full of whiskey. Then he passed it around. The next stop they had SPs [shore patrol] at the station and had us cut off so we couldn't get off the train. We just laughed at it because we had enough liquor to get us to Chicago.

"When we pulled in Chicago they pulled in the Navy yard. They took us to the hospital and checked us in. They gave us orders not to leave the hospital. I went to sleep that night and when I woke up the next morning the hospital was empty. All the guys had taken off for home without any papers. I got a call from the Red Cross that my folks were unable to locate me. They gave me a number and I called them.

"The next day my brother came up and got me and we went home. I didn't have papers, but I didn't care. I stayed home for a month or so and then went back. We were in the hospital one morning and the doctor came in. The waste cans were full of whiskey bottles. He shook his head and said, 'I don't know if you guys are tough or just crazy.'

"I was discharged and sent home a few days later."

POINTS OF INTEREST

Wake Island Firsts

During the defense of Wake Island, the 1st Defense Battalion accomplished the following firsts for World War II:

1. The first enemy surface warship sunk
2. The first enemy ship sunk by American aircraft
3. The first Japanese submarine sunk by American forces
4. The first and only abortive amphibious landing operation
5. The first Medal of Honor awarded posthumously, to Marine Aviator Captain Hank Elrod, and
6. The first presidential Unit Citation and the only one awarded by personal direction and signed by President Franklin D. Roosevelt

Captured and Killed From Wake Island

Killed in action (including 3 Navy)	44	Civilians on Wake	1,200
Total captured	442	Killed in action	82
Died in POW camps (Marines)	18	Died in POW camps	115
Died in POW camps (Navy)	9	Died escaping	2
Number repatriated (including Navy)	415	Executed October 7, 1943	98
Died after the battle	2		
Number repatriated	901		

Civilian POWs on Wake Island

After the capture of Wake Island, the Japanese retained some civilian contractors to finish construction projects. On October 7, 1943, the Japanese marched the 98 prisoners to a location on the beach and executed them with their machine guns.

Nitta Maru

The *Nitta Maru*, which transported the Wake Island defenders to Japan, served as a transport until November 25, 1942, when she was sent to the Mitsubishi Nagasaki Shipyard for conversion to an aircraft carrier. After conversion the *Nitta Maru* was renamed *Chuyo*.

On November 19, 1943, the U.S. submarine *Sculpin* was sunk near Truk. The forty-two survivors were taken to Truk and transferred to the escort carriers *Chuyo* and *Unyo*. En route to Japan the *Chuyo* was torpedoed by the U.S. submarine *Sailfish* and only one of the prisoners survived. He and 20 prisoners in the *Unyo* were taken to Japan.

The first and last duties of the *Nitta Maru* in World War II were as a prison ship.

Legal Claim Against Japan

The Center for Civilian Internees' Rights filed a claim against the Japanese government seeking an apology and compensation for American POWs and civilian internees who were brutalized and mistreated by Japanese Forces during World War II. As of yet, they have been unsuccessful.

— 2 —

SERGEANT ALVEL L. STRICKLIN
U.S. ARMY

---

301 Infantry Regiment, 94th Division
Captured During the Battle of the Bulge
Prisoner of War
January 21, 1945–April 24, 1945
Stalag XIIA and XC

From Farm Boy to Soldier, March 1943

Alvel Stricklin was working on the farm with his father when he turned 18. The war was going full steam and like all young men his age he had to register for the draft. He registered, and two months later he was drafted. Alvel went to Camp Grant, Illinois, for training and was at several other camps before ending up in Texas with Company A, 301 Infantry. His unit went through combat infantry training and on August 6, 1944, his outfit was shipped to Europe.

Northern France and Belgium,
August 1944–January 21, 1945

Alvel and his unit fought day to day for four months against heavy German resistance through northern France. After three Bronze Battle Stars and four months of fighting, A Company, 301 Infantry, stopped near Belgium. The Battle of the Bulge had started on December 16 in the Ardennes region of east Belgium. The goal was to trap the allied armies and negotiate a truce on the western front. Even though the German

Offensive was a total surprise to the Americans, it fell short of the goal. All the Germans accomplished was to create a bulge in the American line. Three days after the offensive began, the American stand-off, along with reinforcements, insured that the Germans would not succeed. By Christmas day the Germans had not even met their interim objective, which was reaching the sprawling Meuse River on the fringe of the Ardennes. What the Germans did accomplish was to expend irreplaceable men, tanks, and material.

The Capture, January 21, 1945

Four weeks later, after grim fighting in bitter cold and snow with heavy losses on both sides, the bulge ceased to exist. The Germans still had not given up. Alvel and his unit were in the trenches trying to advance. He recalled: "The Germans were firing directly at us with 88s and we couldn't move. We were in the Monkey Wrench woods. We were taking a lot of direct fire and the casualties were mounting. It was dark and finally the orders came down that we were to surrender. We learned later that it was the Germans' 11 Panzer Division. We threw our guns down and the Germans took us out to a road. We were told to empty our pockets. I dumped everything I had on the ground and the German soldiers came by and took what we had. They took us one at a time before some officers and they interrogated us. All I gave was my name, rank, and serial number. I just pretended I didn't know anything else they asked.

"The next day we started on a march. Each time we went through a village they would stop and call all the village together. They would applaud because we were prisoners of war. We were lucky compared to many. Many times on the march I saw groups of Jews being marched in the opposite direction. Several times I saw them fall because they were so weak they couldn't walk any further. The Germans would just shoot them like dogs. They would leave them lay and continue on. We walked for the next two weeks until we arrived in Limburg at Stalag XII."

Stalag XII

This transit camp at Limburg, Germany, consisted of a number of concrete block buildings with dirt floors. There was no heat, the roofs leaked, and most of the windows were broken out. A few single story barracks were located in the camp. They were divided into four sections with approximately 20 to 30 men per section. The bunks were three tier. Mattresses were filled with straw. In some cases there were no mattresses provided. Open pits were used for human waste. The camp was infested with fleas, body lice, and other vermin. The food consisted of a watery soup with potato peels on occasion, barley bread, and acorn coffee. At the end of the war the conditions were worsened by overcrowding.

Alvel and the other prisoners were starved. After two weeks of marching with little food they were hoping for something more to eat, but lit-

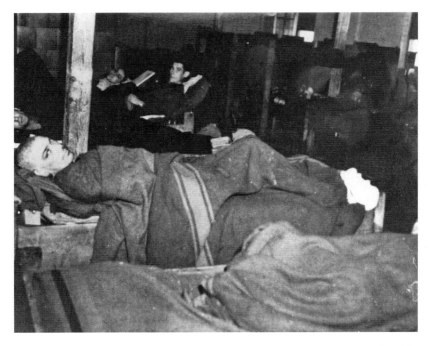

American POWs in the hospital of Stalag XIIA at Limburg, Germany, after liberation on 26 March 1945 (National Archives, Washington, D.C.).

Main gate of Stalag XIIA after liberation (National Archives, Washington, D.C.).

tle changed. They were given some watery soup and a small piece of bread to eat. "We were thrown into a concrete building with straw floors like cattle. There were so many of us we barely had the room to lay down. The straw was full of body lice and fleas. We had them all over us. A couple of days later one of my buddies died. I was on the burial detail. We took him up on a hill and wrapped him in a sheet. He was buried with four other prisoners in the same grave. Then a couple of days later they moved me again."

The Forty and Eight

The Germans took Alvel and several hundred other prisoners to the marshaling yard near Stalag XIIA. The prisoners were loaded aboard boxcars and moved out. "We were jammed in the boxcars to the point that all we could do was sit, one man between the legs of another. We never got anything to eat and only a little water. When one of us had to relieve ourselves we would do it in a helmet and pass it from one person to another until the man next to the air vent could throw it out. Those conditions along with the horse manure on the floor of the train made the smell really foul. Our planes bombed us, not knowing we were POWs, and the Germans wouldn't let us out of the boxcars. We were lucky our train never got hit. We traveled for four days and finally arrived at Nienburg, Germany."

Life at Stalag XC

Stalag XC was in Nienburg, Germany. The usual one-story wood and tarpaper type barracks were used. The barracks had two sections with a washroom in the middle. The facilities consisted of one cold water tap and one latrine hole emptying into an adjacent cesspool. There was a stove in each barracks, but no wood or coal for fuel. The bunks were triple decker. Mattresses full of straw were provided for the bunks. One blanket apiece was issued to the prisoners, but it was not enough to fight against the bitter cold winter. Prisoners huddled together in groups of three or four men to a group to stay warm. The barracks were in a state of despair: roofs were leaking, windows were broken, and there was no lighting. Every building was infested with bed bugs and fleas.

"The conditions at this camp were a little better, but not much. We got soup most of the time, but we got some Red Cross parcels in this camp. They really helped because the thought foremost on all the POWs' minds was food. One day I was looking out this window and I saw this dog coming down the road. Every barracks that it passed prisoners were calling the dog trying to get it to them. It finally went into one barracks and never came out.

"We didn't work at the camp so all we did was wait on time. The conditions didn't help. We all had body lice. I never washed. I never shaved and I had the same clothes on that I was captured in. They had never been washed. It made the days long and the nights miserable. I don't know if I would have made it if I had been captured early in the war."

Liberation and Home

Alvel and the other prisoners were liberated by the British on April 25, 1945. In the three months that he had been a prisoner his weight had dropped from 160 pounds to a mere 89 pounds. He also developed hepatitis and was shipped to a hospital in France. After two months in the hospital he was released.

Alvel crossed the Atlantic by ship and arrived in New York Harbor on June 21, 1945. He was sent home on furlough, and after reminiscing with his family, returned to Florida for rest and recuperation. He was honorably discharged on December 8, 1945.

Battle of the Bulge Facts

1. More than a million men — 500,000 Germans, 600,000 Americans and 55,000 British — participated in the battle.

American prisoners celebrate liberation at Stalag XIIA (National Archives, Washington, D.C.).

SGT. STRICKLIN IS MISSING

Son of Mr. and Mrs. Leo Stricklin Reported Missing In Germany.

Sgt. Orville Lee Stricklin, has been reported missing in action in Germany, his parents, Mr. and Mrs. Leo Stricklin of Stone Fort RFD 2, learned in a telegram received last Wednesday from the War Department.

Sgt. Stricklin, only son of Mr. and Mrs. Stricklin, entered the service two years ago in March and has been over seas several months. He was originally with the Tank Division but had been transferred to the Infantry. He is a nephew of Mrs. Bertha Williams of 710 North Washington Street. Marion.

News report of Sgt. Stricklin's missing in action status (Sgt. Alvel Stricklin).

2. Three German armies, 10 corps, the equivalent of 29 divisions, participated.
3. Three American armies, 6 corps, the equivalent of 31 divisions, participated.
4. There were 100,000 Germans killed, wounded, or captured.
5. There were 81,000 American casualties, including 23,554 captured.
6. The British had 1,400 casualties.
7. On both sides 800 tanks were lost, and the Germans lost 1,000 aircraft.

— 3 —

TECHNICAL SERGEANT THOMAS HAROLD BOARDMAN U.S. ARMY AIR FORCE

96th Bomb Group, 413th Bomb Squadron
Captured During a Bombing Mission Over Germany
Prisoner of War
September 13, 1944–April 25, 1945
Stalag Luft IV

Marriage, the Draft, and the Army, February 1943

World War II affected the lives of everyone, especially young men. Such was the case for Harold Boardman. The war was in full swing and so was Harold when he was drafted in the U.S. Army in February 1943. It was just two months after he was married and two days after his 19th birthday. He was sent to Shepard Field, Texas, for basic training and then to Laredo, Texas, for aerial gunnery training. In January 1944, Harold went to Sioux Falls, South Dakota, for radio training. After several months of training, he was classified as a radio gunner for B-17s.

The Flight to England, April 14, 1944–May 1, 1944

On the morning of April 24, 1944, in questionable weather, Harold and his crew took off across the United States headed for the east coast.

Flying at the assigned 13,000 feet, the crew landed in Iceland to discover only a lot of rock and no trees.

After a night's rest, they took off for Prestwick, Scotland. On May 1, 1944, on a hazy afternoon, the crew landed in Scotland. The men signed some forms, collected their gear, and were taken by truck to Glasgow Railway Station. After a few hours of training they boarded the train for a long ride. Hours later the crew arrived at Stone, England, where they stayed for ten days waiting on assignment.

During the wait Harold and his fellow crew members were taken to an assembly center, where they were allowed to review daily bombing missions statistics and records. It didn't take long for Harold to realize that you would have to be very lucky to complete the 26 missions required before you got a ticket home. The assignment finally came in. Harold and his crew were being assigned to the 96th bomb group of the 413th Bomb Squadron.

The First 18 Missions, June 7, 1944–September 12, 1944

The weather was on the crew's side on the first mission. "Our first mission was on June 7, the day after D-Day. Because of weather conditions we really didn't accomplish very much. Our bomb group had been called back, but we didn't get the call back and flew over France by ourselves. We were lucky it went without incident and returned safely. The only good thing about it was we got to call it a mission."

Throughout the summer of 1944 Harold and his crew completed 17 more missions in France and Germany. They covered a gamut of targets from anti-personnel missions in support of troops, oil refinery complexes, to engine factories. One raid however, is pressed in Harold's memory. "The worst raid I went on was over Paris. We were bombing a Stanford Oil plant on the outskirts of Paris. For morale reasons our bombing route was issued by the Air Force. We couldn't release our bombs by radar so we had to do a visual bombing raid at 17,000 feet. When we finished the bombing raid we returned and flew over the heart of Paris. We lost half of our bombing group after we released our bombs. The Germans had some expert anti-craft gunners and they were accurate. I did three bombing raids over Berlin and expected a good defense there, but it was nothing compared to what we got over Paris."

Mission 19 — The Last Run, June 11, 1944–September 12, 1944

"We often flew with overcast skies. We were not any safer when they used radar to shoot at us, but it made us feel better to have cloud cover between us and the enemy. On our 19th mission we were over Ludwigshaven, Germany, and the clouds dissipated. It was about 12 noon when we moved over the target and there was a clear view of everything. They walked right across our wings with anti-aircraft fire and knocked out three of our four engines. It put us out of the formation and we stayed in the air for about 30 minutes and almost made it to France. The three engines caught on fire and we bailed out at 13,000 feet. Our instructors for parachute training always told us to turn on our stomachs. When I jumped I realized I was on my back with my head down. I spent a few minutes trying to turn over and after the third try I could see the trees. I pulled my cord and my chest chute opened up as natural as could be. Had I been like they said, my chute would have opened in my face.

"We landed right in the middle of an infantry division. They were digging in to stop the American advance. I hit about 30 feet from the top of this hill. I hid my parachute and ran to the top of the hill. When I got there I realized we were in the middle of the German unit. I just sat down. A few minutes later a German soldier came up and wanted to know if I had a pistol. By good advice we didn't carry our pistols and were taken prisoner right away rather than being shot. I told them no."

A POW ... Harold's Story, September 13, 1944–April 26, 1945

"The trauma of being a prisoner was a real adjustment. One day you are living a halfway normal life with the exception of the combat missions, a comfortable bunk, plenty to eat, and then the transformation to a status of POW is startling.

"They loaded us aboard trucks with a 15-year-old armed guard and we headed for Frankfurt. The kid was scared to death and so were we. We were afraid they were going to hit a bump and his rifle was going to go off. We made it though. In Frankfurt they interrogated us first. They knew everything about our crew and really didn't push for too much information. After the interrogation they lined us up against a wall outside and took some newspaper shots."

"Then they put us on a train. I was on it overnight and stopped the next day at a temporary camp. Then about four or five days later they put us back on the train. Beforehand they put me in charge of the prisoners. They wanted me to sign a paper that we wouldn't escape. I told them that I wouldn't do it. I found out from one of the guys that they would take our shoes if I didn't sign it. Winter was coming on and I thought about that and the fact that we didn't know where we were going. Then I thought about it and wondered what in the hell would they do if we tried to escape. It was silly to worry about it and I signed the paper.

"We were on the train for seven days. The conditions were terrible. First of all, the boxcar was supposed to hold 40 men and we had 80 jammed in the boxcar. There was a small air vent at each end of the boxcar so the air was tight. Men had to sit between each other's legs and any one that had to relieve themselves had to do it in a helmet and pass it back until the man next to the air vent could pour the contents out of the helmet. The floor had horse manure and straw on it and combined with that, the men would have diarrhea, the close quarters, and no ventilation to speak of, things got real foul smelling. We got very little water or food during the trip. By the time we arrived at the prison camp it seemed like the trip had taken a year instead of seven days."

Life in Prison Camp

"The camp had a psychopath for a leader. Young Nazi marines ran the first prisoners by bayonet and dogs from the train to the camp, three miles away. They bayoneted over a hundred prisoners, although they did not kill any. They also turned the dogs loose on us.

"I was a prisoner for three days before I could eat. We got hard black bread to eat. You could slice it paper thin and it would stay together. Some said it had aspestia powder in it and some said it had sawdust in it. I couldn't eat for the first three days and three days after I was liberated I couldn't eat, but in between was okay.

"After a few weeks in the camp any food began to taste good. The only thing on your mind was food. I ate bread and soup with an occasional potato peel in it. On February 26, my birthday, I had one raw potato to eat. Potatoes and the barley bread were the only solid food that the Germans gave us. The margarine was remarkable. It stayed together regardless of the temperature. I don't know what it had in it, but it spread better than any of our butter. The guy next to me was always talking about what he wanted to eat when he was released. It was a fried egg with a Hershey almond bar on the top. That used to drive me crazy thinking about that, but I never did try it when I got out.

"The barracks had no heat so we were issued one blanket to fight the cold. It wasn't enough, but better than nothing. We wore the same clothes the duration of our captivity and they were never washed. We had no bathing facilities at all. We were covered with lice and fleas. It was just a miserable experience."

The March, January 1945

"In January 1945 the Russians broke through the lines about 15 miles from our camp. We were roused out of our bunks and given the news the next day that the Russians would be in the camp and the Germans would be gone. We were excited, but warned not to get excited too soon. Two hours later we were called out again. This time the Germans informed us that we had a few hours to pack our belongings. The next morning they moved 7,000 of us out of the camp.

"We marched south for three months. We were strafed by our aircraft a couple of times until they realized we were POWs. After that they would tip their wings as they flew over. We would sleep in barns, fields, and on the road as we moved. We didn't get much to eat as we moved. About the same diet as camp — bread, water, and watery soup. My feet were swollen and covered with blisters from the walking. My boots and socks were worn out and that didn't help, but I was better than some. Several of the men couldn't walk because they were so weak. We helped them along and we didn't lose a one.

"We were lucky compared to the Jews. No matter what direction we seemed to be walking, they were always in the opposite direction. They wore stripped clothing. Those poor people were walking skeletons. Many were too weak to continue walking and the others were too weak to help them. The Germans would just shoot them."

Liberation, April 26, 1945

"Three weeks before we were liberated they switched guards and they were much more civilized to us. For two or three days we would hear small arms fire. We were now moving at night and staying up in barns and fields during the day. The Americans were dropping pamphlets telling the Germans to surrender. They had orders to kill all POWs, but the infrastructure broke down to the point that they knew there was no use.

"We got to this little town and there was an American soldier standing at the edge of the town. He had a uniform on with the neatest creases in it, a pencil mustache and a machine gun laying on his lap. I knew then we were liberated. I had so many lice on me that I could have fallen and they would have carried me the last mile. We got across this river and everybody was throwing their blankets down. I threw mine as far as I could and then found out that we were going to stay there for the night. There were hundreds of us looking all around for our blanket rolls. I found mine and forgot that I had a couple of souvenirs in it — A German beer mug and bayonet."

Camp Lucky Strike

"We slept on the straw that night and the next morning they took us by truck to Halle. They had provisions set up for 3,000. There were 15,000 of us. We stood in line for something to eat all day. I had lost 60 pounds in the prison camp and now I was back on my prison diet. I stood there for at least four hours before getting anything to eat. This guy popped out of the tent and said, 'I need 20 men for KP duty.' I shot out of that line and was right there. He took us inside and we got to eat before we started. Then all we did was start unloading truck after truck of C-rations that they were taking inside and cooking. After a couple of hours of that I thought we needed to give someone else a chance. I stuffed my legs and pockets full of C-rations. I couldn't bend my legs when I walked out of the tent. I didn't have to go to the mess hall.

"I had received a shrapnel wound in my left leg and I got treatment for it. Then a short time later we got the word we were going home."

Homeward Bound

It took about two weeks for Harold and the other soldiers to cross the Atlantic. "When we pulled into New York Harbor on June 29, 1945, it was one of the most beautiful sights I ever saw. I was glad to be home." Harold was on leave for 60 days and then returned to camp. On October 29, 1945 Harold was honorably discharged from the service.

POINT OF INTEREST

In the summer of 1944 the Russians liberated Stalag VI. The Germans moved the airmen from the prison camp ahead of the Russians. The POWs were loaded aboard a German ship, the *Masuren.* For days they were kept below decks in horrible conditions. When the men arrived at their new destination they were taken onto the dock and handcuffed in pairs. A German captain gave the order for the POWs to run. Nazi marines armed with fixed bayonets and Alsation hounds chased after the POWs. Many of the prisoners, because of their physical and medical conditions, were unable to run and often fell. The men handcuffed to them were forced to carry them on their backs. When the Hydekrug Run was over, more than 150 POWs had sustained bayonet wounds, dog bites, and broken legs.

— 4 —

PRIVATE BENJAMIN DUNN
U.S. ARMY

131st Field Artillery Battalion
Captured on Java Island During the Japanese Invasion
Prisoner of War
March 8, 1942–September 2, 1945
Jakarta, Singapore, Burma, and Thailand

The Draft and Teaching School, June 1941

In 1941, Ben Dunn was teaching school. The draft was going heavy and Ben was afraid that he would be drafted in the middle of the school year, so in the summer of '41 he went down to the draft board to see when they thought he would be inducted. "I had a fairly low draft number," Ben explained. "They told me that they thought I would be drafted during the middle of the next school year because they were drafting teachers. I asked them if I could go in now and get my time in. They said I could, so I went in on a June draft in 1941. I went to Camp Roberts, California, and after basic training, I was assigned to a regular army unit at the base."

The Molding of the Lost Battalion,
November 1941–June 1942

In November 1941, Ben left the states and stopped at Pearl Harbor. On December 1, 1941, six days before the attack on Pearl Harbor, he headed west with a convoy of nine ships headed for the Philippine Islands. On

December 7, they heard that Pearl Harbor had been attacked and within a day so had Wake Island, the Philippine Islands, and all the other islands in the Western Pacific. Ben's ship headed for Australia; they were the first American troops to land there in World War II. Ben's ship stayed for about a week and the troops had a great time. "Out of all of the nine ships I don't know what happened to them. We were the only one of the nine that had stopped at Australia," Ben said.

"There was one battalion, the 2nd Battalion from the 131st field artillery out of Texas, detached from the 36th Division. My battery was the Brigade Headquarters battery, the 16th Field Artillery Brigade. They took the 2nd Battalion and 120 men from my outfit, put us on a Dutch ship and sent us to Java. We were told that there were submarines in the area, but the trip was a pleasant one. I never saw anything that was a threat. We arrived at Soerabaja, Java, the second largest city in the Netherlands East Indies. Then they moved us about 30 miles from the city to a Dutch air base. There were no planes at the base, but a few days later what planes were left of the 19th bomb group, which had been bombed at Clark Air Base in the Philippines, landed at the base. There were a number of us that were assigned to the Air Force to help with the planes. I learned to fuel planes and load bombs.

"The officer in charge was Colonel Eubanks. He told us the first day we were there that we were going to be bombed by the Japs because there was nothing to stop them. He said, 'Remember to take cover and lay down. Don't stand up at any time we are being attacked.'

"Within a week about 27 Jap bombers attacked the air field and destroyed four of our bombers. The rest of the bombers were out on a mission so they didn't get them. They only killed one native during the raid. He was running for cover and we yelled at him to get in a hole, but he couldn't understand English. None of the military personnel got a scratch.

"This went on day after day. We didn't know what was going on with the war and then one day I got orders to be transferred to the Texas Battalion. There were 17 of the 26 of us from the field artillery that got orders to the 2nd Battalion. The rest of the men went back to Australia.

"In the meantime, the Japanese were headed for Java. The allied fleet wasn't organized. The command was under a Dutch commander and there were some Dutch ships, Australian ships, and an American cruiser. They all met the Japanese fleet as the Japs headed for Java. It was the biggest Naval battle since World War I. Most of the allied ships were sunk, but a few got away."

The USS Houston

The HMAS *Perth*, an Australian cruiser, and the USS *Houston* were ordered back to Australia. The two ships, already damaged from previous battle with the Japanese, limped into Tanjong Priok Harbor, the port of Batavia, to take on oil and make emergency repairs. On the night of February 28, 1942, they left the harbor, made their way through a mine field, and ran head on into a Japanese invasion fleet in the Sunda Strait northeast of Java. The invasion fleet was supported by an aircraft carrier, two heavy cruisers, several light cruisers, two squadrons of destroyers, and dozens of other support ships. They put up a hell of a fight against the Japanese before they were sunk.

Three hundred and sixty-eight crewmen from the USS *Houston* made it to shore and were captured by the Japanese. One hundred and fifty died in the water trying to make it to shore, and over half of the crew went down with the ship. Little did the captured crew know that a short time later they would join Ben's unit and become known as the Lost Battalion.

The Surrender ... Java, March 8, 1942

On March 1, 1942, the Japanese landed troops on both ends of the island. The defense against the Japanese was next to none. The native troops were abandoning the invasion area in large numbers. The Australians were putting up a good fight against overwhelming odds, but were being all but annihilated. The American forces were constantly being delayed by Japanese superior air attacks. The Dutch Air Force and Navy were destroyed and most of their ground troops were natives who were sympathetic toward the Japanese and had deserted. The Japanese couldn't be stopped.

On March 8, 1942, Ben and a group of soldiers were camping in a bamboo grove. They were preparing to continue to the Tjilatatjap port on the southern part of the island to board a ship. One of the officers came by the grove and told the soldiers that it would be impossible to reach the port. Ben and his fellow soldiers were told to lay down their arms and surrender. The Dutch had surrendered the island to the Japanese.

It was a real jolt for the soldiers, but with tear-filled eyes they followed orders. "We didn't know what to expect from the Japanese, but if we had known what was in store for us we would have probably gone into the jungle and resisted," Ben said. "After the Japs arrived we did find out really quick that they put out rewards to the natives if they found someone who escaped. With them being sympathetic toward the Japs we would have been unsuccessful. My morale was really low. We had been captured and had put up no fight at all. I really felt bad about that.

"The Japanese didn't know what to do with all of us prisoners of war. They didn't believe in surrendering. The stories that I heard from the men that fought against them in the islands said they would run directly into a machine gun knowing they were going to be killed because they believed they would be killed by the emperor and go straight to heaven. Since they hadn't expected so many prisoners they hadn't considered the food supply. We would soon learn that we were going to be on a rice diet.

"Here we were, prisoners in Java. We were moved several places at first, but none of the locations were actually prison camps. Once we were at a race track for about a week. They took us up to the mountains to an old plantation. There were about five hundred of us that were in the battalion and they captured us pretty much intact. They moved us around and then finally in May 1942 we ended up in a prison camp in the docks of Tanjong Priok. We worked on the docks doing all kinds of work. We were eating small portions of rice with very little meat mixed in with the rice. It just wasn't enough to eat, especially with the forced hard labor.

"One of the worst things at first was trying to get used to their regulations and their language. We couldn't understand Japanese. We got orders in Japanese and, according to their standards, if we disobeyed they could beat us, slap us or hit us with a butt of a rifle if we didn't follow orders. It wasn't long before we learned to count in Japanese and to sound off in Japanese. We learned Japanese orders. If a Japanese soldier came by, regardless of rank, we were required to salute or bow. In their eyes we were the lowest thing on earth. In the morning if a Japanese lieutenant got up and didn't feel good, he might slap a sergeant around, then the sergeant would beat up on a private and the private would beat up on the prisoners. We worked at hard labor on the docks for about six weeks being slapped, beaten, yelled at and starved. Then they moved us again."

The Bicycle Camp, June 1942

In June, Ben's unit was moved to downtown in Batavia, now given the Indonesian name of Jakarta. They were marched from the train station to an old military Dutch camp called the Bicycle Camp. "This camp was completely encircled by a high barbed wire fence with a single asphalt street running down the middle of it from one end to the other. Four parallel barracks were located on both sides of the street. The first three barracks on the right from the entrance to the camp were for American prisoners of war. The other barracks on the same side of the street were for Dutch officers and civilians. The barracks on the other side of the street were occupied by the Australians, except for the last barracks, which was used as a hospital. The mess hall was behind the Australian barracks.

"All the buildings were permanent with running water taps near each building. There were no bunks in the barracks, so each prisoner found their own spot to sleep."

The Japanese guard house was located just inside the entrance to the camp on the left side of the street. The porch was always crowded with Japanese guards armed with rifles and fixed bayonets. No one knows the reason why the camp was named Bicycle Camp, but the name was of little concern to the prisoners. The camp would prove to be the best Ben was to live in as a prisoner of war. "It was a better camp then any we had been in. We had electric lights and a couple of outlets. When we got there, there were Americans already in the camp. They were in bad shape. They were half naked and had sores all over them. They were the survivors of the *Houston*. There were 368 out of the 1,100 man crew and they were all in this camp. They were starved. We had some supplies and we started sharing our clothes and blankets with them. We became one unit and some of us would spend the rest of the war together. We were the Lost Battalion.

"In a couple of months they started moving prisoners to Japan. All the Navy officers had been sent earlier and then they sent out the colonel and some more officers to Japan. Myself and the other prisoners worked on the docks, built an airport, worked in a rubber plant, and worked in a Japanese headquarters where they were getting auto parts from cars they had taken from their captures.

"At this time the food wasn't too bad. The rice was cleaner, but the rice we got when we were first captured was dirty. I think it had been swept up off the floor. It had bugs in it and worms. For a while some of the guys wouldn't eat it because it made them sick. When you get hungry, you start eating and after a while everybody picked what bugs and worms they could out of the rice. As time passed we just ate the rice, worms, bugs and all. Once in a while we got a vegetable and a piece of meat. We ate everything we could get our hands on.

"We had a radio and since we had electricity we would listen to it. The Japs didn't know it but some of the guys took it apart and rigged it and we were able to get some news once in a while from San Francisco. The officers told us to sign whatever they wanted us to because it didn't mean anything because we were signing it under duress. If we wanted to try to escape we could. We signed the papers and they quit beating up on the officers.

"They wanted to find out how many technicians they had, so they give us some papers to fill out. Some of the guys put down the truth and some didn't. Some of the Australian prisoners put down that they were beer tasters. Some of the Americans put down that they were peach fuzz removers. The Japs took about 60 of the men that they thought were technicians and they shipped them to Japan. We never saw them again until the war was over.

"In another month they took 200 more prisoners and two officers and they shipped them out. We didn't know where they were going. Later we found out that they were shipped to Singapore and then to Burma to work on the rails."

The Dai Nichi Maru, *October 1942*

In October 1942, the Japanese loaded the remaining Americans and Australians aboard the hell ship *Dai Nichi Maru.* "We were down in a hole packed in like rats." Ben explained. "It was hot and lucky for us it was a short trip. We didn't have enough water to drink. They gave us a little cup of rice twice a day. Most of us weren't hungry. It stunk so bad that we couldn't eat. Men were sick and throwing up. The Japs wouldn't let us clean it up. Everyone had dysentery and if you had to use the bathroom you had to go up on the deck and sit on a wooden stool that hung over the edge of the ship. You were sitting out over the ocean and the stool wobbled and shook. We were afraid that it would collapse and if we fell in we were dead because the Japs wouldn't try to help us. As a result, most prisoners relieved themselves where they sat."

Twelve days later the ship pulled into Singapore. It was a welcome sight for Ben and the rest of the prisoners.

Singapore, October 1942–January 1943

Ben was taken to a large, sprawling camp in the low hills on the east end of Singapore. It had permanent stone barracks that had been used in peace time by the British army. The prisoners slept on the concrete floor and again picked their own spot.

The camp was surrounded by barbed wire fence and the Japanese guards were posted on the outside of the fence. The camp consisted of English, Scots, Gurkhas, Indians, Australians, and now American prisoners of war. The Japanese had captured about 100,000 British troops in Singapore, Malia, and the islands up and down the area. About 60 thousand troops were in the camp when Ben got there. The Japanese turned over the interior operation in the camp over to the British. The Japanese guards were on the outer perimeters, and on occasion they would come in and check things out.

"The food was terrible," Ben said. "We got dirty rice and rotten vegetables to eat. One day I walked over to a basketball court where some British officers were trying to play ball. In 1942, the British didn't know anything about basketball. They asked if I knew anything about basketball. I told them I played a little and they asked if I could get some friends and play them a game. The next day we met and played. We beat them 50 to nothing. After the game was over, the British took us in their barracks and gave us some tea. I looked around and there were cans of food from the Red Cross sitting on their chairs and shelves. They had taken the Red Cross packages and kept them for themselves while we were eating rotten food. We told the other prisoners what we saw and needless to say the American and British prisoners didn't get along from then on. We would be walking along and see a British officer coming along and we would act like we were going to salute them. They would snap to attention and salute as we were raising our arm, then we would scratch our head. They would report us to our officers, but they wouldn't do anything."

The Journey to Burma, January 1943

After about three months, on January 6, 1943, Ben and about 350 Americans packed their gear and were marched to Singapore and put on a train for Georgetown. To their horror they were loaded on another hell ship, the *Moji Maru*. "The conditions were worse than the first ship, partly because we were on it longer," Ben said. "We were headed north for Burma. There were two ships. We were within a day of arriving at Burma when we were attacked by American planes. I was sitting down in that hole and I looked up through that hatch and I saw planes. The bomb bay doors opened and here came the bombs. Two bombs hit really close to the ship and it started to list. We thought it was going to sink but we couldn't get up out of the hole because the Japs had machine guns on us. The planes left without making a second run, but they had sunk the other ship. A bomb hit right in the hole where the Jap soldiers were. The soldiers on top went overboard. There were some Dutch prisoners on that ship and they went overboard. The Japs had life jackets, but prisoners weren't given life jackets. When we picked up the survivors some of the Dutch prisoners had on life jackets. They told us that the soldiers went into the water with their rifles, helmets and packs. They could hardly move. The prisoners would swim up to them and hold them under until they drowned, then take their life jackets."

The Death Railway, January 1943–January 1944

The death railway was not yet in the vocabulary of any of the prisoners. It was a project that even the Japanese engineers had said was impossible. Yet, by the command of the emperor the project began. The railroad was to run from Ban Pong, Thailand, to Thanbyuzayat, Burma. The Japanese were building the railway to get much needed supplies to their troops on the India front. It had been in operation only three months when Ben arrived, and it would be one year later before the railway was finished. It took more than 300,000 men in 260 miles of mountains and the most diseased jungles of Thailand and Burma to build the railway. The toll it took on those men resulted in the railway being named the Railway of Death, and would be burned into the memory of the POWs who survived.

Thanbyuzayat was the jumping-off place for most of the POWs and Ben was no exception. He listened to the speech by Lieutenant Colonel Y. Nagatoma that had been repeated over and over to the new groups of POWs brought to work on the rails:

"It is a great pleasure to see you at this place, as I am appointed chief of war prisoners camps in obedience to the imperial command issued by his imperial majesty, the emperor. The great East War has broken out due to the rising of the East Asiatic nations whose hearts were burnt with the desire to live and preserve their nations on account of the intrusion of the British and Americans for the past many years. There is therefore, no other reason for Japan to drive out the Anti-Axis powers of the arrogant and insolent British and Americans from East Asia in cooperation with our neighbors of China and other East Asiatic nations to establish the Greater East Asia Co-Prosperity Sphere for the benefit of all human beings and to establish everlasting peace in the world.

"During the past few centuries, Nippon has made extreme endeavors and sacrifices to become the leader of the East Asiatic nations who were mercilessly and pitifully treated by the outside forces of the Americans and British, and Nippon, without disgracing anybody, has been doing her best up till now for fostering Nippon's real power. Therefore, you are now only a few remaining skeletons after the invasion of East Asia for the past few centuries and our pitiful victims. It is not your fault, but until your government wakes up from their dreams and discontinues their resistance, none of you will be released. However, I will not treat you badly for the sake of humanity, as you have no fighting power at all.

"His majesty, the emperor, has been deeply anxious about all the POW camps in almost all the places in the southward countries. The imperial thoughts are inestimable and the imperial forces are infinite, as such you should weep with gratitude of them and should correct or amend the misleading and improper anti–Japanese ideas. I shall meet with you hereafter, and the beginning of various times. Although there may be lack of material, it is difficult to meet all the requirements.

"(1) I heard that you complain about the insufficiency of various items. Although there may be a lack of materials, it is difficult to meet all your requirements. Just turn your eyes to the present conditions of the world. It is entirely different from prewar times. In all countries and lands, materials are considerably short and it is not easy to obtain a small piece of cigarette or a small match stick and the present position is such that it is not possible even for the needy women and children to get sufficient food. Needless to say, therefore, that at such inconvenient places, even our respectable Nippon Army is not able to get mosquito nets, foodstuffs, cigarettes, and medicines freely and frequently. As conditions are such, how can you expect me to treat you better than the Imperial Japanese Army? I do not persecute according to my own wishes and it is not due to the expense, but do to the shortage of materials as such distant places. In spite of my wish to meet your requirements, I can't do so with money. I shall, however, supply you if I can do so with my best efforts and I hope you will rely on me and all you render your lives before me.

"(2) I shall strictly manage all of your going out, coming back, meeting your friends, communications, possessions of money, and other things shall be limited. Living manners, deportment, salutations and attitude shall be strict and in accordance with the rules of the Nipponese Army, because it is only possible to manage you all who are merely remnants of a rabble army by the order of military regulations. By this I shall issue separate pamphlets of house rules of the war of POWs and you are required to act strictly in accordance with the rules.

"(3) My biggest requirement from you is escape. The rules for escape shall naturally be very severe. This rule may be quite useless and only binding to some of the POWs, but is more important for all of you in the management of the camp. You shall, therefore, be contented accordingly. If there is a man that makes one percent chance at escape, we shall make him face the extreme penalty. If a man is foolish to try to escape, he shall see big jungles toward the east which are absolutely impossible for communications. Towards the west, he shall be faced with boundless ocean, and in all points and most important, our Japanese Army is staying and guarding. You will easily see the difficultly of complete escape. A few such cases of ill-omened matters which happened in Singapore shall prove the above and you shall not attempt such foolish things, although it is a last chance after your complete embarrassment.

"(4) Hereafter, I shall require all of you to work, as no one is permitted to do nothing and eat as a prisoner. In addition, the Imperial Army had great works to promote at the places newly occupied by them and this is an essential and important matter. At the time of such shortness of material, your lives have been spared by the military and all of you must reward them with your work. By the hand of the Nipponese Army, railway work to connect Thailand and Burma have started to the great interest of the world. These are deep jungles, where no man comes to clear them by cutting trees. There are almost countless difficulties, but you should do your best efforts. I shall check carefully and investigate about your non-attendance, so all of you should, except those who are really unable to work, be taken out for labor. At the same time, I shall expect all of you to work earnestly and confidently every day. In conclusion, I shall say to you, 'work cheerfully,' and from thenceforth you shall be guided by this motto.

"Lt. Col. Y. Nagatoma

"Chief No. III Branch

"Thai War Prisoners' Camp"

Ben couldn't believe it. How could they possibly do it? It was impossible. For the next year he would work daily with one thing in mind: Survival. And against all odds he would survive.

"We made it into Moulmein, Burma, on January 16, 1943. That was the beginning of our experience on the railway of death. They took us to a place called Thanbyuzayat, which was the jump-off place for building a railroad that was to connect Bangkok, Thailand, with Rangoon, Burma. It would be 260 miles long and run through the jungles and mountains. The reason they were building it was because the Americans were sinking the Jap supply ships that were trying to get into Burma. The Japs had an army ready to attack India, but had to hold them up because of a lack of supplies. This railroad was being built to get those supplies to them."

18 Kilo Camp

"This camp consisted of several huts. They were made from bamboo and leaves from the jungle. In these huts we chose our spot on the floor and that is where we slept. They put us to work on this railroad nonstop. We were divided into groups of fifty. There was usually a second lieutenant in charge and we also had the Jap guards. We built this railroad without any machines. I never saw a machine until after the railroad was complete. It was picks and shovels and wheel barrows. The first group of American prisoners that had arrived before us had cleared the jungle and we were the dirt moving group. We had picks and shovels, but no wheelbarrows. We carried dirt in a basket. When they told us what we were building, I couldn't believe they thought we could build it with no equipment. Each day we marked off the area we were to cover. At first we started out with 1.2 cubic meters. We knocked that out and would go back to camp and eat rice. We didn't have enough water and we had to boil it. It was hot so we would go back to the camp and boil water and drink all we could. I drank the hot water. I never had a good cold drink of water for three and a half years. This work was what we did day after day.

"Then they moved up the area to two cubic meters a day. That was the beginning of really hard work. The Dutch prisoners told us not to finish the work as fast as we could so we could get back to camp to rest, but to string out the work because the Japs would just keep adding more area to work on a daily basis. They were right and we slowed down the work.

"It was really hot out there picking and digging. Some of the ground had really gotten hard. This was in the beginning and some of the pris-

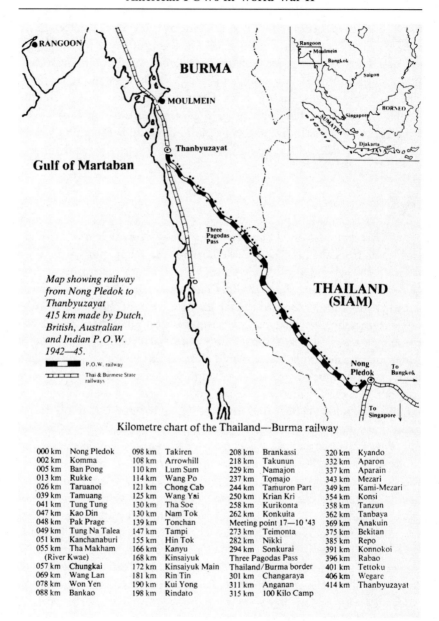

Kilometre chart of the Thailand—Burma railway

000 km	Nong Pledok	098 km	Takiren	208 km	Brankassi	320 km	Kyando
002 km	Komma	108 km	Arrowhill	218 km	Takunun	332 km	Aparon
005 km	Ban Pong	110 km	Lum Sum	229 km	Namajon	337 km	Aparain
013 km	Rukke	114 km	Wang Po	237 km	Tomajo	343 km	Mezari
026 km	Taruanoi	121 km	Chong Cab	244 km	Tamuron Part	349 km	Kami-Mezari
039 km	Tamuang	125 km	Wang Yai	250 km	Krian Kri	354 km	Konsi
041 km	Tung Tung	130 km	Tha Soe	258 km	Kurikonta	358 km	Tanzun
047 km	Kao Din	130 km	Nam Tok	262 km	Konkuita	362 km	Tanbaya
048 km	Pak Prage	139 km	Tonchan	Meeting point 17—10 '43		369 km	Anakuin
049 km	Tung Na Talea	147 km	Tampi	273 km	Teimonta	375 km	Bekitan
051 km	Kanchanaburi	155 km	Hin Tok	282 km	Nikki	385 km	Repo
055 km	Tha Makham	166 km	Kanyu	294 km	Sonkurai	391 km	Konnokoi
	(River Kwae)	168 km	Kinsaiyuk	Three Pagodas Pass		396 km	Rabao
057 km	Chungkai	172 km	Kinsaiyuk Main	Thailand/Burma border		401 km	Tettoku
069 km	Wang Lan	181 km	Rin Tin	301 km	Changaraya	406 km	Wegare
078 km	Won Yen	190 km	Kui Yong	311 km	Anganan	414 km	Thanbyuzayat
088 km	Bankao	198 km	Rindato	315 km	100 Kilo Camp		

The route of the Thailand-Burma Railway (Pvt. Benjamin Dunn).

56

oners started getting sick. They came down with malaria. I knew what the symptoms of malaria were because I had it as a kid when I lived on the Mississippi River. It is hard to describe what malaria is like, but you get really hot and almost feel like you are crawling. It goes in stages: first there is the high temperature and then heavy sweats. Another thing about it is that it will go for four or five days and you think you are over it and then it comes back. I had it come back on me approximately 30 times while I was a prisoner. I was working one day down in the pit and I started feeling it come on me. I stopped working and went over to the side of the pit and sat in the shade. I knew that quinine would knock [out] the malaria and we had that in the camp. That night I took some quinine and the next day, I could go to work. Different ones came down with it and it really hit some of them hard.

"Every day we would walk to the point where we were working, work all day, and then walk back to camp. The next camp from us was 12 miles so the more we worked the longer the walk each day. We would go back to camp and boil water and drink all we could hold so that our bodies were saturated for the next day's work. We had been told that the food at Burma was going to be better than in Singapore and we were looking forward to it. When we got there, it was better. We got rice with as much as an ounce of meat in it and more of it for the first two weeks, but the work was so much harder."

85 Kilo Camp and 80 Kilo Camp

"In the middle of May 1943, they took us by truck to 85 Kilo Camp. That was 50 miles from the main base camp and it was deeper into the jungle. It would be the last time we would be moved by truck. At this camp there was a stream running down the middle of the camp and we could use it to bathe and to get fresh water for boiling. It didn't last long, though, because we did the same kind of work for about two weeks then they moved us again."

"We started to work at this camp [80 Kilo Camp] and we were there until the end of June. It was terrible. By now we had to walk 12 miles to get to the working area. The food was getting worse and there was less of it. Many of the guys were sick with malaria, dysentery, and just weak from the hard work and the lack of food. The healthy ones helped carry the sick to work. We never lost anyone. Then they moved us again."

100 Kilo Camp

"It was at this camp [100 Kilo] that the rainy season really started. The first day in the camp we had one of our prisoners to die on the railroad. The work was really hard here. We had to work in the mud and rain. They cut our food rations in half with no meat and the men started dying fast. One food item we had was a melon. It looked like a watermelon, but it was white. They gave those to us and we cut the melons up, boiled them, and ate them with our rice. They had no vitamins or food value at all. The Australians called the melons 'white death' because when we were put on a diet like that prisoners started getting beri beri. That is a disease caused by vitamin deficiency. It started in the face or sometimes in their scrotum and it would swell many sizes. Then finally it would get in the lungs. A person's lungs would fill with fluid. You would hear your friends gasping for air because of their lungs filling with fluid and you knew that they weren't going to live. Within a few hours they would die in their own fluid. All of us had a little bit of joint disease from vitamin deficiency. Most had malaria.

"Then if you worked out and you got a cut on your legs it would get infected and cause tropical ulcers. It was a sore that would start eating on the flesh until it would get to the bone and then it would spread out. If you had them long enough, it would even affect the bone. We had two doctors, one from the *Houston* and the other from the 131st battalion, but they didn't know how to deal with it because they never saw a disease like that. The guys would take rags, soak them in water and put them on the sores, and try to soak that rotten flesh out. They would do that every day, but it didn't heal them. When they really got bad, the men would be taken back to the base camp and the Australian doctor would amputate. They lost more than they saved. The American doctors with us operated on a few and didn't save any.

"The group of Americans that had arrived in Burma before us were luckier than we had been. Every one of the 200 Americans in that group had a tropical ulcer of some kind. They had a Dutch doctor with that group who had lived in the jungles all his life. He had a sharpened spoon that he used to dig the rotten flesh out of the ulcers. He didn't lose a single prisoner.

"I had malaria and amebic dysentery. You don't get rid of it without proper drugs and I didn't have any drugs. Our doctor died. Right before he died, he told me that I couldn't get out and work on the railroad any longer. He told me to stay in or it was going to kill me so I stayed back and when the men that could work left the camp the Japanese would send one of our officers down to the barracks and make everybody that could walk go outside. This major came through one day and asked me what was wrong, 'Can you walk?' I told him hell, yes, but I'm not going to because the doc told me to stay in here and I'm going to. He told 'em it was up to me. But there would be a Jap soldier that would be coming through with a club soon. Pretty soon this Jap came by and asked me what was wrong. I told him malaria, beri beri, and dysentery. He felt of my forehead and I must have had a temperature because he went on and never said a word. They would asked some what was wrong and they would say they couldn't walk. The Japs would take them outside and beat them. They had nine prisoners out once and beat them with bamboo poles. They would hit them in their ulcers which made them grow faster. I don't know if they did it to make them die faster or not, but they did die faster.

"On the job you would always look to see who was going to be the guard, because some were worse than others. We had one we called Liver Lips. He was dark and big and when he got mad and started beating on a prisoner it seemed the more he beat the madder he got. We had another guard called Mocon. Mocon was a word for food and he was always around the kitchen looking for food. He didn't like me for some reason. I found out later that they did not like blue eyes. They called them fish eyes. I had fish eyes."

Operation SPEEDO

"They started Operation SPEEDO. The work day got longer and the work got harder. If you were sick, they cut your rations in half. It didn't matter for the Americans because they shared anyway and soon everyone got less food. Then they decided to send the sickliest men back to 80 Kilo Camp, where we had been before. By this time that camp was run down. This was at the end of the rainy season in the fall of 1943. Every day they would take a truckload of sick prisoners to this camp. They were taking them there to die. My name was on the list but I told them that I didn't want to go, I could walk. A friend of mine who had been through all of this with me saw me getting on the truck and came up and said, 'Dunn I just came from 80 Kilo and it is worse than this camp. You don't have to work there, but you don't get as much to eat. It's bad there.' I explained that I had no choice, the Japs were sending 25 today and 20 the next day. They told me I had to go. The Japs paid us ten cents a day and he gave me a dime and told me that maybe I could buy an egg or something with it. I told him he needed it as badly as I did, but he insisted. I got on the truck and when we arrived I couldn't believe it. There were only four or five men that could walk in the whole camp. The rations were half of what we had gotten at Kilo 100. Men were dying like flies.

"There were two other Americans that could walk. They were orderlies. I could walk and we did the best we could to take care of each other. I found out that over the past three months 61 Americans that had been sent down to this camp had died. It was a combination of things that killed them. They all had malaria, beri beri, dysentery, tropical ulcers, and they just gave out.

"I found two of my friends in this camp. We had been in Camp Roberts in the States together. They both had tropical ulcers, malaria, and dysentery. Every day I would go down and visit them. One of them had the worst tropical ulcer I ever saw. It went from the ankle up the leg with the whole shin bone showing white. They both lived through that and I think it was because they were so close. They supported each other and I went down every day to help them, too. They were in a ward at one end where the prisoners with dysentery were. Each day when I would go down I would ask where some prisoner was. 'Oh, he died. We buried him yesterday.' It was really demoralizing.

"One of the native Dutchmen showed me a plant in the jungle that was good to eat. The Japs only had two guards and they rarely checked on us. They knew we weren't going any place and they didn't like the smell in the barracks so they didn't come there either. I could walk about 30 yards before resting so I would slip into the jungle and pick some of these plants. I boiled them and ate them with my rice. It helped some. I also checked the Japs' garbage and picked out what we called Harry Carrie. They were a little tube that was about as big as my thumb. I threw them in the fire and roasted them and then ate them. One day I was roasting some Harry Carries and I asked one of the Americans who slept by me if he wanted a couple of them. He said he did. I took them out of the fire and he said, 'they are kinda burnt aren't they?' I said, yeah if you don't want them give them back. He said, 'Oh they are just the way I like them.' He died later.

"The two other Americans that could walk were busy every day burying the dead. I had just returned one day from burying some prisoners and the Japs told us we were moving out. The railroad was finished."

Kilo 105

"They put us on boxcars and took us to Kilo 105. While I was there, I had the worst attack of malaria that I ever had. Every time my heart would beat a really sharp pain would go right down my spine. I thought to myself, here I have made it through all of this and we are about to get out of here. Am I going to die now that I have gone through all of this? All night long that sharp pain was there. The next morning the pain was gone. Even though it was hot, I stood by the fire all day. We found out that the prisoners that had stayed in the camp while the railroad was being built had a Cholera epidemic and most of them died. Why they brought us back into that camp is beyond me. Maybe they thought we would die. We stayed there for a few weeks and then they moved us again."

"They put us on a train and [we] made a trip from there into Thailand. It was really exciting. That railroad was crooked and shook. All the prisoners tried to sabotage the railroad as it was being built. They would put stumps in the footing so it would eventually rot out. If they put a bolt in the track and the Japs weren't looking they would take the nut loose. Anything to make the thing fall apart, and in places it did."

The "Death Railway" at Chong Kai, Thailand (Pvt. Benjamin Dunn).

Camp Tamarkan

"We made it to Thailand on January 4, 1944, stopped at the Kwai Bridge, and camped there. Most of us couldn't work, but things began to get better because of the Thai people. The Thai people were good. Anytime they had prisoners of war in Thailand the Thai people would aways try to get food to them. I got a lot of duck eggs in this camp. The food was better and many of us started to get better. None of us got well until we got out of the camps, but we started to get better.

"There were several thousand of us in the camp and I was there when the Americans bombed the Kwai Bridge the first time. I was in the malaria ward, which was the first hut by the bridge. One morning they came in and moved us to a hut at the other end of the camp because I had malaria. The Americans came in that day and bombed the bridge. They missed the bridge and the bombs hit this hut that I had just been moved out of and killed 17 Australian and Dutch prisoners. It was right where I had been sleeping. They bombed the bridge several more times, but every time they missed it.

"We were there for several months. They gave us a glass rod test to check for amebic dysentery. If you didn't have dysentery or malaria at the time, they put us on a list to go to Japan. By that time it was 1944 and it wasn't safe in Japan. I had amebic dysentery. With amebic dysentery you think you have to go to the bathroom all the time. All you will pass is a handful of blood and pus. Since I had the dysentery, I wasn't going to Japan."

Camp Nakhon Pathom, February 1944–March 1945

Ben had survived the Death Railway and was slowly recovering from the terrible conditions at those camps. Then things even got better. He was sent to another camp. "It was the best camp that I had been in Thailand," Ben explained. "It had huts with wooden floors in it that we slept on instead of the bamboo slats. The barrack was built better and was supposed to have been a hospital. There were a lot of doctors, but no medicine. The Japs had received medicine from the Red Cross packages, but they would not give it to the doctors. At one time there were 7,000 sick prisoners in this camp. I was there five or six months and I started getting better. The food was better. The Thai people would get as much food as they could to us. The only work I did there was haul wood a couple of times. Also, they built a brick wall around the camp and I worked on that some. They had a workshop where they were making artificial legs. Some of the prisoners worked in them and they were helping each other, making limbs for each other and it helped rehabilitate them.

"Slim Chambers was in this camp with me. He was funny. I don't care how things got in the camps, he always had something funny to say. He would make up jokes about something I did or something someone else did. It was really good that we had someone like that.

"A guy by the name of Dempsey Key was in my battery and we became good friends. He could steal more things from the Japs than anybody I ever saw. When we were in Singapore one time, the English officers had a bunch of chickens in a pen. They weren't giving anybody the eggs or chickens but the other officers. Key sneaked down to the pen and stole nine of those chickens, pulled their heads off, and laid them at the back door of the officers' barracks. The officers blamed it on the Japanese.

"Many of the prisoners' joints were stiff because of weight loss. When you weigh say 170 pounds and you go down to 80 pounds or so your muscles and joints get stiff. In this camp one of the doctors got a group of healthy prisoners that went around and did rub downs on other prisoners and tried to help them learn to walk again."

The Kawi Camp, March 1945–May 1945

"By now it was the Spring of 1945," Ben said. "They started shipping us out if we were well. I was in pretty good shape except for a little dysentery, so I was shipped back to the camp on Kawi. I was only there for a couple of weeks and went through a couple of bombing raids and they finally hit the bridge. A couple of weeks later they put us on a train and took us to Bangkok. There we were put on a barge and started down the river. I thought for sure they were taking us to the ocean. We are going to Japan. I thought about trying to escape because I saw the B-29s going over. I knew it would be dangerous. Well, we stopped along the river and they took us to a warehouse where we worked for a few days."

Camp White Pagoda, May 1945–July 1945

"They put us on another train and sent us to Ratburi, where they were building an air field. I worked there and then at a rock quarry. I hauled wood and kept the fire going. There was a school near us. One day we went by this school and looked in it. We saw a picture drawn on the blackboard with planes dropping paratroopers. We thought it meant something, but we didn't know what. It did mean something because the Thai people were always trying to tell us something, but we didn't understand their language.

"Every night there were planes flying over real low and dropping supplies and weapons to the Thais to help fight the Japs. The planes were from the Office of Strategic Services. They were supplying them to help for the big invasion. They were to take over all the prison camps and release the prisoners. The Americans knew that the Japs had issued orders that in the event of invasion that they were to destroy all records and kill all POWs. The Thai people were trying to tell us, but we didn't understand them. The Korean guards saw the end of the war coming and they wanted to take care of themselves. They told us that they had orders to kill all of us if there was an invasion. They told us that almost every day and I could hardly believe it. They told us that if we wanted they would take us to the Americans, but we didn't believe them. It was only a couple of months before the end of the war. Finally a couple of guys took off. They took them to OSS and American officers were there and got them back to American hands.

"They moved us next to some mountains and we started digging holes in the side of the mountains for the Japs to hide in. We were carrying ammunition and food on poles to the positions. One day they sent us out to feed some Jap soldiers. They had a basket on a pole and we started out. It was about two miles across the rice paddy and I could smell the food. I looked in the basket and it was boiled duck. I started eating on it and I told the other guy that he better get some. By the time that we got there we had eaten almost all the duck. We dropped the basket and ran back across the rice paddy in the dark. I always wondered what happened to those Japs when they opened up that basket and found nothing but bones.

"The next day we were outside the tent waiting on the Japs to tell us what they wanted us to do. One of them came out and told me to pick up a 200 pound bag of rice and take it across the rice paddy. I couldn't pick up a 200 pound rice sack. Even in my best days I couldn't have done it. When I was younger if someone put it on my back I might have been able to carry it. We had never heard this group of Japs say a word in English, not a word. I knew that he knew I couldn't carry it. We were all getting pretty cocky and I said carry it yourself you son of a bitch. He said, 'don't call me a son of a bitch.' Then he hit me up side the head with a bamboo pole. One prisoner that was with me took the pole away from that Jap. I told him that we were in for it now, they are probably going to shoot all of us, but the Jap went back into the tent and didn't say a word."

Nakhon Nayot—The Last Camp, July 1945–September 1945

"We were sent to our last camp. We worked a couple of days and then about the third day in camp we went out to work. We got about a quarter of a mile from the camp and the guards stopped us. We sat on the side of the road, they gibbered a bit, and then took us back to camp. They told us we were going to have a rest day. We wondered what was going to happen and we wondered if the war was over. That night the Japanese guard house had a bunch of sake and kee and some other prisoners stole the sake and a bunch of prisoners started drinking. The next morning at roll call half the prisoners were drunk. The Jap officer took the soldiers out and beat them with his sword for letting the prisoners steal the sake. That day we didn't do anything and we still didn't know for sure what was going on, but we soon found out."

Liberation, September 2, 1945

"The next morning when we got up the Japanese were gone. We had a formation and this British officer stood before us and said, 'This is the happiest day of my life. The war is over.' We started yelling and slapping each other on the back. Some cried, but Chambers was standing beside me. He was about as big around as a sick peach tree. He looked at me and said, 'God damn Dunn, I'm getting to get home in just enough time to pick cotton.'

"We all sang our national songs. Then the next thing you know the English, Australians, and Dutch had their flags up. I don't know where they got them, but we didn't have one. We got the liner of some of the English tents, the red from the Dutch liners out of their hats, and a white lining I had and made a flag. It took us two days to sew the flag, but when we raised it, it was the most beautiful thing I had ever seen.

"It was August 17 when they told us it was over and it had been for a couple of days. Then the Japs started coming by in trucks. They were drunk and had lost their discipline. We heard shots fired and thought they were probably killing themselves, but we were told not to fly our flag for a few days.

"A week later the Americans came in and got the American POWs. The English, Australian, and Dutch couldn't believe we were leaving that quick, but they took us to a big hospital in India. We had white sheets, pretty nurses, good food, and a lot of care. It was really hard to believe that we had made it through the imprisonment and that we were really free."

Home, October 1945

Ben was in the hospital for several weeks before returning to the Walter Reed Hospital in the States. After being assigned to Ward 35, he called his parents. It was the first time that Ben really felt free.

After a couple of days, one of the officers came into the ward and told the men that the president would like to have a group from the 131st unit to come to Washington to the White House. The officer looked at Ben and asked, "How about you Dunn?" Ben had heard too many rumors and said, "No, I'll take a rain check. Just tell Harry I'll drop in some other time."

The next day Ben picked up the newspaper and saw pictures in the paper of his buddies at the White House with the president and his family. They were having a great time. Although Ben had wished he had gone, he was happy for his friends who had been entertained by the president.

On October 13, 1945, Ben arrived home. His parents were at the train station and although they had aged and had developed noticeable lines from worry, they looked great to Ben. Ben's parents saved all the newspaper clippings and magazines during the war. Ben had a chance to catch up on the war. All the major battles and events were new to him. To this day Ben still reads of events in World War II that he had not known about.

POINTS OF INTEREST

Catching Flies

The Death Rail prison camp became so infested with flies that the Japanese ordered the prisoners to catch 100 flies each night. The Japanese guards would come around with a bucket. If the guard thought that you had enough flies to make 100, he would let the prisoner put them in the bucket. If he did not think the prisoner had not caught 100 flies the Japanese guards would beat him with bamboo clubs.

Construction of the Railway

For 13 months, prisoners of war and local natives constructed 260 miles of railway from Rangoon, Burma, to Bangkok, Thailand. The path of construction took them over some of the most rugged mountains and through some of the most diseased jungles in the world. The Railway of Death was completed without the use of a single machine.

Lives Claimed

The Burma Railway of Death claimed the lives of over 130,000. Although the actual account is difficult to determine, some historians have estimated that as many as 393 men died for every mile of track laid. Approximately 26,000 of those were allied POWs. The remainder were native prisoners.

A Failed Railroad

The Japanese overestimated the ability of the railway. It was able to ship 600 tons of supplies daily to the India front. This was only one fifth of the estimated amount. In November 1944 information supplied to Americans by recovered POWs resulted in intensified bombing on the railway. It became inoperable within months of its completion.

Bridge on the River Kwai

The movie *Bridge on the River Kwai*, released in 1957, won seven Academy Awards. The movie tells the story of World War II British POWs captured by the Japanese and forced to build a bridge over the river Kwai. Colonel Nicholson became obsessed with building the bridge. In the end he saw the bridge finished, only to have allied commandos blow it up just as the first Japanese train was crossing over. The truth is that there was no

Colonel Nicholson, there were no allied commandos, and the Kwai bridge still stands today.

After the war was over the Allies sold the Kwai River bridge back to Thailand. The proceeds were divided among all the prisoners of war. Each prisoner received about $280.

— 5 —

SERGEANT WILLIAM ROBERT CARR
U.S. ARMY

398th Bomber Group, B-17 Gunner
Captured After Being Shot Down on
a Bombing Mission Over Germany
Prisoner of War
August 4, 1944–April 26, 1945
Stalag Luft IV

A Call to Duty, September 1942

Bob Carr was excited when he entered the U.S. Army on September 10, 1942. He always had an interest in flying and he received orders for the glider program. After his basic training he was transferred to Texas and completed 30 hours of glider training, but to his surprise, the Army decided to disband the program. They said they didn't need any more glider pilots. "The Army gave me a choice; I could be discharged and drafted later or I could take my choice of training as a crew member for a B-17. The training would consist of radio or engineer school. I chose radio school and was shipped to Rapid City, South Dakota. I wasn't the best radio operator. I could only take on 20 words a minute and I got beat out of a spot by a man who could take 22 words a minute.

Then they sent me to gunner school in Yuma, Arizona. I had to take training as an aerial gunner. I was then sent to Rapid City, where I was assigned to a crew. I was there for about six weeks and then sent by train to the East Coast, and we shipped out a few days later. The next day we were in a big convoy."

Early Missions

Bob and his crew landed in Liverpool, England, on July 14, 1944, and were assigned to the 39th Bomb Group, 601 Bomb Squadron Group. The crew trained for about two weeks in their newly assigned B-17, the Hells Bells. Then as Bob tells us, they got their first mission. "My first mission was on July 28, 1944, Sourbergenon, Germany. It was rough, but we made it through all right. We didn't have any Messerschmitts after us, just flak from the anti-air craft guns. There were a few planes that went down in our group, but we didn't take any hits at all. The next two days were bad weather so we didn't fly."

The second mission they weren't so lucky. "Our next mission was scheduled for August 3rd. It was over Holle, Germany. Our navigator got wounded on this mission and on our return we had to break formation going back. There was an ambulance waiting when we got back and I thought, well we won't fly tomorrow. I was wrong."

Being wrong wasn't the worst of it. It would be the last mission he would fly in the war. "We had a mission on August 4th and were flying over the Baltic. We acted as if we were going further over the Baltic, and flew past the target, then made a right angle turn and came back over the target. Things were uneventful until after we dropped the bombs. One of them hung up. We worked on it and got it to drop. About that time some flak hit us. I was unclear as to the damage and all I can remember is what the radio operator said, 'That sounded like a bunch of rocks being thrown on a tin roof.' Immediately we were on fire and the left Tokyo tank was burning. The pilot called me on the radio to see if I could see anything underneath because I was in the ball-turret. I couldn't see anything, but the decision was made to drop down to 10,000 feet from the present 24,000 to see if could put the fire out. We dropped down and got the fire out. The pilot then discussed with the navigator if we should try to fly across the Baltic sea to Sweden. It was about 74 miles, but it was across water, so they decided not to chance it. Shortly after that, the fire alarm went off again and orders were given to bail out. I had put my parachute under my left arm in the gun turret that day so I decided to bail out from that position. It was an uncommon way to leave the plane and as I started out I caught my side pockets on the plane and had to climb part way back in. Then I jumped. As I was falling, I watched the plane head over the Baltic Sea and take a nose dive. The fall was uneventful, but as I got close to the ground I could see people coming from all directions. When I landed, I was trying to take my parachute off."

The Capture, August 4, 1944

"One of the home guards, a man about 45, was riding his bicycle across the field as fast as he could. When he got up close to me, he said, 'Pistola, Pistola.' I said no. He pointed a pistol at me. About that time two Polish farmers came up carrying pitch forks and pointed them at me. The home guard ran them off. I found out later that there was a reward of 10,000 marks for any capture.

"He then took me across the field to his house. It only had one room, but the most amazing thing to me was that the door to the house led out to the chicken house and the chickens could walk in and out of the house freely. I was standing in the room watching his wife and two daughters take the parachute apart for the silk material. Then all at once a hand grabbed me from behind and threw me out into the yard. It was the burgermiester of the town. He was very angry. He started hitting me and asking me questions in German. I didn't know any German so I didn't answer him. He beat on me for a while and then he started taking all my clothes off. He found an escape kit in one of my pockets. It had maps, money, and some food. I had forgotten about it coming down because I saw all the people gathering before I hit the ground. Anyway, he went ballistic and started beating me again. He took me into town and had me stand in the road as he took the rest of my clothes off except for my briefs. There were women standing all around me. Then one of the home guards came up and he got into an argument with the bergermeister. They were face to face yelling at each other. I don't know what was said, but my guy won because the bureremieister gave me my clothes back and I got to get dressed."

The Journey to Prison Camp

"The home guard took me down a little trail through the woods to a road that led to another town. We were doing all right for a while and then we passed a guy on the road who was carrying a shotgun. He stopped the home guard and they started talking. They got into an argument and I thought I was going to get the worst, but then the home guard motioned for me to start walking. We continued on and as we would pass farm houses people would come out and take turns hitting me with their fists. I got smart and started putting myself between the home guard and the people until we finally reached the town. The Germans had knocked out the side of a basement wall in a house and used it as a holding place. That's where they put me and to my surprise part of my crew was there. It wasn't long until a bus came and got us.

"We went by a B-17 crash site. The pilot of the plane was still laying out in the field. People were going up to the body and kicking the body just to see if it would move. One of the captured crew members from that crew told us the pilot had held the plane steady until all the members could bail out. I couldn't believe the unconcern that the people had that were kicking at the body. They were full of hate.

"Soon we arrived at the airfield. Once again I had to take my clothes off. The Germans went through them and asked a lot of questions. I had to strip all the way this time, and because I had been circumcised they wanted to know if I was Jewish.

"We stayed the night and the next day they loaded us on a train. It was a passenger train and there were German soldiers on the train going home on leave. They didn't pay much attention to us. They were all happy I suppose because they were going home. We passed through Berlin, and unfortunately for us we did so right after a bombing raid. We had stopped at the train station and had gotten off the train and walked to another train a couple of blocks from where we were. There was a crowd gathered and they were throwing rocks. The soldiers were protecting us, but just as we got to the other train one of the Nazi soldiers came up and hit one of the pilots in the face. I'll never forget what the pilot said: 'You son-of-a-bitch, if I get loose I'll come back and bomb you again.'

"One of the guards handed the radio dispatcher that was on the train a satchel to carry and one of the civilians tried to grab it out of his hand. Just about that time we were starting to board the train and a man was standing on the platform beside us. He could speak English very well and he said, 'You bastards. You dirty bastards.' The radio operator looked at him and said, 'Blow it out your ass.'"

The Interrogation

The Germans brought all the American pilots through Frankfurt for interrogation. Bob was no exception. "We arrived in Frankfurt, Germany, and they took us off the train. There was a bus to take us up to the interrogation center, but our bus was too small and we had to walk. The German sergeant was pressing us hard, and some of the guys had shrapnel wounds so they couldn't go any faster. He seemed to be pretty good until he had an audience and then he had to show his authority. Once no one was watching he would let up on us.

"We arrived in late afternoon. I got my picture taken and then they took me for interrogation. I gave my name, rank, and serial number and that was all. They told me they were gong to give me some food in a little bit, but I didn't get any food that night.

"The next morning they gave me a slice of bread and some peas. They interrogated me again. Because I had been separated from my crew, they thought I was a P-38 pilot instead of a B-17 crew member. There had been some P-38s shot down in the area. We went back and forth for a long time, me giving my name, rank, and serial number and them asking about being a P-38 pilot. This went on for about three days and the last person to interrogate me was a Nazi major. He asked me about my position and I gave my name, rank, and serial number. Then to my surprise I learned he knew all about my crew. He named each position on the plane and even knew the crew members by name and position. I respected him for one thing. He knew that I was in the ball turret, but he wouldn't make me say it."

The Train Ride

"The next day we were sent by train, forties and eights, to Stalag Luft IV in Poland. The train ride took five days. We got little food and no water.

The conditions were terrible. There was no room to lie down. Men had to sit between each other's legs. There was no place to relieve yourself so men were relieving themselves in a helmet and passing it across from prisoner to prisoner until the prisoners by the vent could dump it. The smell was unbearable. On several occasions they stopped in larger towns in the marshaling yards for bombing raids. They locked us in the train. Every bomb they dropped we thought was going to drop on us and they came close enough that we had flak hitting the top of our car. It took five days to get to the prison camp, but it seemed like five years."

Stalag Luft IV

Stalag Luft IV was located at Gross-Sycrow, Pomerania, 20 kilometers southeast of Belgard. This prison camp did not open until May 12, 1944. The barracks were wooden with insufficient ventilation. Bathing facilities were inadequate. The toilet facilities consisted of a row of toilets and an open pit behind the barracks. The barracks were surrounded by barbed wire.

The adjustment to prison life was a shock for American prisoners of war, especially pilots who often just days earlier were living normal lives other than the bombing missions. "Stalag Luft IV treatment was very rough. When our planes came over, the Nazi guards would go ballistic. They would make us go inside the barracks. We weren't supposed to look out. One of the guys got close to a window and saw the guard aim at him just as he moved away from the window. The window was shot out. I was there until January and I got one shower. We got one piece of bread a day and soup once a day. The Red Cross sent us packages, which helped. The packages were supposed to be for one person, but four of us had to share one package.

"Each morning we were required to fall out in front of the barracks. Sometimes they would pick at random one barracks and trash it. They would throw everything out in the middle of the floor and when you went back in you had to find your things. They claimed they were looking for a radio.

"One day a group of four German planes came over. All at once one plane took a nose dive and crashed into the ground near the camp. The Nazis went nuts again and made all of us go inside. They started test firing guns, which made us really nervous."

Abandoning Camp, January 1945

In 1945 the Russian front was moving fast. It was closing in on the prison camp and as many of the camps did, they moved the prisoners. "About the middle of January we started hearing artillery fire in the distance. It was the Russians making a drive. The Germans told us to get our stuff together, that we were going to move out. We would walk about 10 or 15 kilometers for the first couple of days. They always tried to keep us in a building of some kind, and one of the nights that building happened to be a chicken coop.

"We all got lice really bad. We would try to sleep for a while before the lice woke up and started moving. When they did move they would bite and we had red splotches all over our bodies.

"We walked and walked. When we would come to a larger town, we would see tin foil on the ground where our planes had dropped it to mess up the radar. We had been told not to talk to the civilians. These people had been in war for at least three years and when we got into the war many of them had either been bombed or had family killed in the war and may retaliate against us. As a result, the guards said they would not be responsible for our safety if we spoke to anyone.

"We weren't getting much to eat. Bread and water was about it. One day we were on a break standing next to the side of the road. It was in the Baltic area and it was wet and muddy. This man came by in a carriage with horses. It looked like something that you see in the South during the 1800s. He had been wounded and was on his way home. He said something to the people that were with him and they dropped some of the potatoes on the ground for us. We ate them that night.

"I had dysentery bad. It's hard to explain how you had to drop your pants in the middle of town or where other people were to relieve yourself, but there was nothing else you could do. There was a Canadian doctor that was with our group and he sent word down the line to eat charcoal.

I got a stick and built a fire. I ate the charcoal. It was easy to do because I was hungry. It stopped the dysentery. I found out later that it was a common way to relieve dysentery in the States. The air raids were getting closer all the time. Then we began to see observation planes. We started walking in PW formation to let them know we were prisoners of war. We thought we were doing pretty good. A formation of B-29s came over and I looked up. I thought, that looks like a pretty good formation. Then I noticed that the bomb bay doors were open and I saw these little dots dropping. I realized that they were bombs. A building near where we were was hit. The building had been a storage building for captured materials that Germans were keeping. Each of us got a bayonet and I put mine in my coat. I carried it for the remainder of the war. Occasionally, we would hear planes firing in the air, but all we could see were vapors, then a parachute where a pilot was coming down.

"We knew that it was about over and when we started coming by houses with white bed sheets hanging out their windows; we had no doubt the war was about to end."

Liberation, April 26, 1945

"About a day before we were liberated, we had a change of guards. The old guards had sometimes been bad, hitting on us and so forth, so they gave us a new guard that walked with us for about a mile, and some of the British that had been captured for up to four years began to take the rifles from the guards. We walked to the lines and were liberated on April 26, 1945, at Bitterfield, Germany. We walked across the bridge at Bitterfield. My feet were bloody from the shoes that I had been wearing. They didn't fit. We went to an aid station and they cleaned me up. We were really hungry. I had lost about 35 pounds. I can remember the big pile of K-rations, and we were trying to get through this fence to get to them. This major came along and got on top of them with his pistol drawn to keep us from getting into them.

"Later we moved to Holte, Germany, and I had a chance to take KP duty. I found some fresh cans of fruit and some condensed milk. I ate and drank and it stayed down for about ten minutes. I was really sick. It took a few weeks to get my system used to the proper diet.

"A couple of days later they put us on a DC-3 and flew us to Camp Lucky Strike in France. We were fed every day three or four times a day until we were sent home."

Homeward Bound, May 30, 1945

On May 30, 1945, Bob and several thousand other ex–POWs boarded a troop ship and headed for the United States. About two weeks later, on June 13, 1945, they arrived at New York Harbor. Bob took leave home, returned to the Army for the rest and recuperation, and a few months later, on October 29, 1945, was discharged from the Army.

POINTS OF INTEREST

Airman Over Europe

From 1939 to 1945 during bombing raids over Nazi occupied territory, 150,000 allied airmen were killed. Another 45,000 were captured and approximately 6,000 were shot down and evaded capture.

Prison Slang in the Stalags

Goons — The name the POWs gave the guards and staff in their respective prison camps.

Ferrets — The name for the German guards who roamed the camp's interior searching for escape attempts or contraband.

Going into the bag — A British slang term for being taken prisoner.

Round the bend — A term for a POW that was experiencing psychoneurosis (irrationality or depression). Initially a British term adopted by the Americans.

CORPORAL KENNETH M. SMITH
U.S. ARMY

Company H, 423rd Infantry Regiment, 106 Division
Captured During the Battle of the Bulge
Prisoner of War
December 19, 1944–April 2, 1945
Stalag IXB

A Day in Infamy, December 7, 1941

Ken Smith's story begins on Sunday afternoon, December 7, 1941, as a sixteen year old boy. It was a beautiful day. Ken and his brother came into their house, and from the look on their father's face, the two brothers knew something serious was going on. Ken's father was listening to the old Zenith six volt battery operated radio. He told the boys that the Japanese had just attacked Pearl Harbor and told them to sit down and listen to it because it was going to affect all of their lives. "I don't know what happened to me at that moment, but I can remember it as if it was yesterday. I knew I would be in the military as soon as I was old enough. I wanted to be.

"I was 16 and had already quit school, and I worked for an oil contractor. I worked most of the time until my 18th birthday, which was January 25, 1943. About a week later I went to the draft board and told them I wanted to be in the next bunch that was going in. In March they called me up. I wanted to go in the Marines. They sent me to Chicago for my physical and told me that the Marine quota was full. I asked for the Navy and I got orders for Scott Air Force Base. I thought, well, that won't be too bad to be in the Air Force, and after I got to the base I got another set of orders and two days later I was headed for Fort Jackson, South Carolina, for Army Infantry. They were just activating a new division: The 106th Infantry Division."

Training with Company H, March 1943

Ken was assigned to a heavy weapons unit, H Company, 423rd Infantry Regiment. He felt fortunate to be in a newly formed unit because everyone was equal. Basic training was a little more demanding than Ken thought it should be. "I was fighting the system for about the first three weeks because I thought it was a little tougher than I was. I had a platoon sergeant, Sergeant Webb. He called me into his office one night. He said he wanted to talk to me. He told me that I was just going to make it harder on myself by rebelling and talked with me for a long time to try and change my attitude. I am glad he did because I did change my attitude and at the end of training I was promoted to corporal."

Orders came down that a number of men were going to be taken out of the outfit and sent overseas as replacements. Ken had enlisted to fight and he volunteered to be a replacement, but they turned him down. Instead he went into advanced training and finally ended up in the Tennessee mountains on maneuvers. Ken was ambitious and an excellent soldier, but once again he ran into trouble. He and a lieutenant got into a disagreement and in the end Ken was busted back to private.

AWOL

It made Ken so mad that he went to a bar, got drunk, and went over the hill. "I had some friends in Indianapolis and I went and stayed with them. I worked for thirty days driving a truck for Roadway Express under my friend's name and social security number. After that I went back home to Mt. Carmel, Illinois. The chief of police saw me and told me that I if I didn't get out of town he was going to arrest me because he had a warrant. I left town and went back to Indianapolis. Three days later I was walking down the street and I saw a mess sergeant from H Company. The unit by now had moved to Adebury near Indianapolis. I asked how things were going. I knew I had to go back, but I didn't want to be caught. I still felt a duty to my country, but I had made a mistake and I didn't know how to correct it. I decided I would turn myself in to the company hoping that it wouldn't be as bad on me. I caught a bus back to Adeberry and walked into the barrack. The first sergeant was sitting behind his desk and I said, "First sergeant, I want to turn myself in." He looked at me and said, "Smith, my ass bleeds for you." Then he told me to go over to a certain barracks and we would take the matter up the next morning.

"The next morning the company commander called me in. He had all my records. Up to the time that I went over hill I had a good record. He wanted to know what made me do such a thing. I probably wouldn't have done it if I hadn't been drunk, but he told me that he would have to court-martial me. He would go as light as he could. I had a special court-martial and I got six months at hard labor and loss of two-thirds of my pay. They took me back to the barracks. I didn't have any gear and I was waiting for them to take me to the stockade. About two hours later the runner came over and took me to the captain's office. He had all my records out on his desk and he went over some of them. Then he saw where I had volunteered to go overseas. He asked me if I still wanted to go. I told him that's what I joined the Army for, and he told me that he was going to send me to replacement. He would suspend my sentence, but I would still lose my pay. I was relieved and went back to the barracks still under guard. A short time later he called me back to his office. He told me that there was a problem, that he couldn't send me overseas without a furlough. I swear to God, I was home on leave five days later.

"When I got back my orders were delayed and I was sent in a motor pool. I worked there most of the summer and by fall we got word that the entire unit was being shipped overseas. We had some proficiency test that we had to take. The captain came and got me and wanted me to take a squad for the test. We had our water cooler machine guns and the way it worked we would set up fire at targets until we were told to advance. We did this in three stages. I wanted to do something for the captain since he helped me and I worked my butt off. We got the highest score and that was the end of my motor pool days. I was back in the infantry as a gunner."

Crossing the Atlantic, October 1944

On October 8, 1943, Ken and his unit left Indianapolis by train and two days later they were in Massachusetts. Then after eight idle days, on October 16, they boarded a train to New York harbor and boarded the *Queen Elizabeth*. Five days later they had crossed the Atlantic and landed in Scotland. October 24 they boarded a train for a trip to Totington, England, where they stayed until November 17.

Born, Belgium, December 1, 1944–December 15, 1944

On December 1, the 423rd loaded aboard LSTs (transport ships) and started across the English Channel. The LSTs returned to England a short time later, however, because of engine trouble. Five days later repairs were complete and the unit crossed a rough English Channel and landed in France on December 5. The men were moved from there in open trucks in the rain and four days later made it to Born, Belgium. Companies G, H, and Headquarters remained in Born while Companies E and F were moved to the nearby village of Medell. These companies were in division reserve. The rest of the outfit had moved up on the Siegfried Line.

Thinking the Ardennes was the least likely spot for a German offensive, American staff commanders chose to keep the line thin, so that the manpower might concentrate on offensives north and south of the Ardennes. The American line was thinly held by three divisions and a part of the fourth, while their division remained in reserve. As Ken recalls, it was a big mistake: "even in training today an infantry division is only capable of covering over a three mile front. The 423rd regiment alone was covering a seven mile front. One battalion in the 424th was in reserve in another town. The 422, 423, 424 were covering a 26 mile front of the Siegfried line. There hadn't been any action in that area for weeks. During the time from December 11 to the 16th, 1944, it was obvious that there was a big buildup going on behind German lines. Reports were going back hourly about what was going on, but it was all being ignored."

The battle that was to begin on December 16 was Hitler's last gamble. He sent three powerful German armies plunging into the semi-mountainous, heavily forested Ardennes region of eastern Belgium and northern Luxembourg. The goal was to reach the sea, trap four allied armies, and impel a negotiated peace on the Western front.

Battle of the Bulge, December 16, 1944–December 19, 1944

At 5:30 A.M. on December 16, the Germans started their offensive across the rough forested and rocky terrain. It was bitter cold. Snow mixed with rain was falling from the overcast skies. The 423rd Regiment was right in the middle of it. The first German outfit that hit went around the unit. Ken recalled: "We were ordered to move up and set a defense to secure the roads north and east from Schönberg, Germany. We did and were set up on the roads by evening. The cavalry and engineer units that had positions at Andler and Auw begin making a fast withdrawal. They were moving headed toward Schönberg."

December 17

Early in the morning Ken's unit began to receive heavy resistance. "We lost a lot of men that day. We were ordered to move up the road and support 589th field artillery battalion, which was under heavy attack. Their trucks and guns were stuck in the mud and the Germans were going to overrun them. So we attacked and got all of them out with everything but two guns. By that time we had lost communications with the division. We were trying to get the artillery unit back to St. Vith, Belgium, but every road we tried was either too muddy or filled with German tanks.

"Somewhere [near] Auw, Germany, we were trying to break through the German lines. We were moving down a very muddy road. We just had a few riflemen with us because everything was in chaos. No one knew what was going on. The front of our column hit heavy resistance and we were ordered to get off the road. My platoon sergeant, Sergeant Webb, told me to take two men and check out these two houses that were along the road, to see if there were snipers in the houses. The Europeans build their houses with a barn in one end and living quarters in the other. We went through the barn and there were cattle in the barn. We went into the kitchen and the stove was still warm, but there was no one around. The house was clean and neat. We went upstairs. There were big beds upstairs. They were neat and the floors were shiny. I was a farm boy and the house reminded me of home. The guy with me said he was going to lay down on the bed and I told him that if he did I would shoot him. He looked at me really funny when I said that; I guess I had a serious look on my face, but we did leave the house as we found it.

"We went back to the road and we could hear real heavy fighting ahead of us. We went on down the road with our squad jeep and we got about a half a mile down the road from the house. We went around a slight curve to the right and there was an open field to our left and to our right. This lieutenant that I had had trouble with in Tennessee was now the executive officer of the outfit. He came up and got me and told me to set up my machine gun along this fence row about two hundred yards from where we were located. There was an open field in front and I saw there was about a platoon of Germans grouping together along the edge of the woods. I waited until they got in place and I opened up. I think I got most of them. I emptied a two hundred and fifty round belt. There was a lot of yelling and screaming going on. Then a mortar shell hit out in front of me about fifty yards. It didn't do any damage, but I knew what was coming. A few seconds later there was one landed just behind me and it must have been a concussion shell because I didn't get any shrapnel, but the concussion almost knocked me out. I picked the gun up, tripod and all, and headed for the jeep. The column was just starting to advance ahead. The jeep was full so I threw the gun on the tongue of the jeep. We took off and myself and the gun fell when we hit a bump. I hit hard and I really hurt my shoulder. I was lucky, though, because a few seconds later the jeep was hit and everyone in the jeep was killed. Then the Germans started pushing the column back. We couldn't hold them so we moved back where the houses were [that] we had checked."

December 18

By the morning of December 18, Ken's unit was being attacked from both sides. The fighting was fierce and the casualties were high. They moved into the Ardennes forest and lost contact with the Germans. That night they bedded down in the forest. It was bitter cold. Heavy snow mixed with rain fell from the skies. But Ken and his fellow soldiers, exhausted from the three days of fierce fighting, paid little attention. They laid in the mud all night trying to sleep.

The Capture, December 19th

As daylight broke on the morning of December 19, Ken's unit came under heavy artillery fire. "It was tree burst. It was terrifying. Men were getting killed everywhere; just blown to bits. We had joined with the 422th division and the commander had already sent a delegation to the Germans to surrender to. One colonel told the commander that he didn't have the authority to surrender his unit. We were going to fight our way out. We thought we could but we would never have made it, and because the com-

Prisoners from the Battle of the Bulge being marched to prison camp, in a photo taken by the Germans (National Archives, Washington, D.C.).

mander of the 422 outranked the colonel, he had to surrender. He did tell us, though, that if any of us wanted to try and get out that we could.

"Myself and eight other guys took off through the woods toward the artillery because we figured we could run under it. And we did get out of the artillery fire. We ran through the woods for about two miles and felt like we could get away. We came upon this road and I found out later that it was a road coming directly out of Auw, Germany, which was one of the main roads the Germans were using. We came up on this road and as far back as you could see there were troops, tanks, and horse drawn artillery. Anything you could think of. We were laying there trying to figure out what we should do when a German motorcycle with a side car on came wheeling up. A German officer stood up in the side car and spoke perfect English. He told us we were surrendered. If we didn't come out of there they were going to blow us out.

"We found out later that they had a 20 millimeter trained in on us down the road. By now I had lost my machine gun. I had picked up an M-1 rifle, three rounds of ammo and three hand grenades. We had lieutenant Thomas with us and he asked us what we wanted to do. The majority wanted to surrender, but I didn't want to. I had my gun aimed right at this German officer's head. I wanted to blow his head off and to this day I wish I had. We surrendered. Lieutenant Thomas kept saying, 'Don't Smitty, don't Smitty.' We threw our weapons down and walked down the hill with our hands up. It was the saddest day of my life. That wasn't what I joined the Army for. It was just an absolutely horrible experience to do that.

"They marched us down to the road. There were a few other prisoners down there. They didn't search us, but told us to empty our pockets. I still had three hand grenades in my pocket and I threw them down. They immediately picked them up. I threw a can of c-rations on the ground and they got them. The only thing I had left was a pocket full of Teaberry chewing gum and Chesterfield cigarettes. I had forgotten that I had them. I had gotten them the day before when I was looking for a pair of boots when we were on the jeep. I had gotten into this duffel bag looking for the boots and I found a carton of Chesterfield cigarettes, a box of Teaberry chewing gum and a fifth of Scotch whiskey. We had drank some the night before and then finished the rest of it the next day going through the woods. I had forgotten about the cigarettes and chewing gum, but they let me keep them.

"We started marching down the road and every once in a while we would pick up more prisoners as they were captured and assembled in different areas. By nightfall there was over 500 of us. We knew then that it had been a major offensive. We walked way into the night. We finally stopped and I laid down in the ditch. It was muddy and snow was on the ground. I reached in my pocket and discovered that I still had a hand grenade in my pocket. I talked with a couple of the other prisoners and asked what we were going to do. One suggested that we wait until a car full of German big shots came along and throw it on them. We figured that we would get a bunch of people killed doing that, so we finally decided we would dig a hole and bury it. That's what we did."

The Journey to Prison Camp, December 20–24, 1944

The next day, December 20, the prisoners walked all day and arrived that night at a small village, where they stayed in a bombed out building. The Germans gave them each one small, two-inch-square biscuit. That's all they had to eat since the day before they were captured.

The next day the POWs walked 18 kilometers to Geraldsden, Germany. "It seemed a lot longer," Ken explained. "There they loaded us on boxcars. There were 70 men in each boxcar. Not enough room to all sit down. If you sat you had to sit between someone else's legs. Before the train moved out one of the German soldiers yelled out, 'escape.' He opened fire knowing the boxcar was packed. One soldier was killed. Then we moved out. When we had to relieve ourselves, we went in a helmet and it was passed to someone on either end of the boxcar where it was dumped out of the air vent. It got pretty rank in there. We had been loaded on the 22nd and on the night of the 23rd we were sitting in the railroad yard at Limburg. A plane came over and dropped an incendiary bomb. We had a pilot on our car and he told us that we were really in for it because that was just a sight for the bombers to follow. He was right because shortly they bombed us. We were lucky our car wasn't hit, but there were some killed. The next morning, I don't know how they got that railroad repaired, but they did and they pulled us out of there. We would go a little ways and stop. A little further and stop. Then after four days we arrived at Bad Orb."

Stalag IXB

The prison camp was located in Hessen-Nassau region of Prussia, 51 kilometers northwest of Frankfurt.

Each barracks had 290 to 500 men assigned to it. The barracks were one story wood and tarpaper types divided into two sections with a washroom in the middle. Washroom facilities consisted of one cold water tap and one latrine hole emptying into an adjacent cesspool which had to be shoveled out every few days. Each half barracks contained a stove. Throughout the winter the fuel ration was two armloads of wood per stove per day, providing heat for only one hour a day. Bunks, where there were bunks, were triple deckers, arranged in groups of four. Three barracks were completely bare of bunks and two others had only half the number needed. As a result, 1500 men were sleeping on the floors. Some bunks had mattresses and some barracks floors were covered with straw. The straw was used in lieu of toilet paper. The outdoor latrines had approximately forty seats, insufficient for the needs of 4,000 men. Most prisoners reserved one blanket, but because of overcrowded conditions, supplies ran out and several hundred of the prisoners had no blankets. All the barracks were in poor condition, roofs leaked, windows were broken out, and lighting was either unsatisfactory or lacking completely. Only a few barracks had tables and chairs. Every building was infested with bedbugs, fleas, lice, and other vermin.

Christmas 1944

"On Christmas day we arrived at a little town of Bad Orb, Germany," Ken recalled. "We were unloaded off the train and started walking up this little mountain road and finally arrived at Stalag IXB.

"We stood outside in the rain and cold until each one of us was interrogated individually. Although we didn't give anything other than name, rank, and serial number, there was no need in getting smart with them because they already knew everything they needed to know about us. One of the things that we remembered during training was that if we were captured it was still our duty to do what we could to cause trouble for the enemy. If we could do something to keep one extra man busy that would be one that couldn't fight. I always kept that in mind and I was sort of mouthy anyway."

The Escape Plan

"I behaved for a while and then me, Bobby Lee, and a couple of other guys started planning an escape. It didn't seem like it would be hard to get out of the place. Every night before they would lock us up in the barracks they would line us up in rows of five and count you off. I figured we could cause some confusion in the court for a couple of days. We figured that we needed to get someone out at night so we could see what was going on and then plan our escape. Myself, Lee, and the guys messed up the count. The Germans finally got tired of messing with the prisoners so they let us go back in the barracks. That night we found some place that looked pretty good for escape. Some of the places didn't look like they would be much digging to get under the fence. There was a barbed wire fence, about ten feet of rolled wire and then another barbed wire fence. We figured we could make it if we could figure out where the guards were.

"Well, someone must have been offered extra food and believe me there wasn't much of it because we were found out."

The Beating

"They took our whole group of sixteen men and put us in a little building. It was used as a recreation building where they could play some games. We had to sleep on the floor because we were branded as troublemakers. When an American died we were made to bury them. They also made us cut wood for the German quarters across from the camp. One day we were cutting wood and this German officer came by and was yelling at us. I never looked up from cutting wood and said, 'You Kraut eating son of a bitch.' One of the other German soldiers could speak English real well and he told the officer what I said. The German officer said something to the other German soldiers and the next morning I woke up in the barracks badly beaten. I mean real bad. I couldn't hardly move for three days. I thought I was going to die. My chest hurt so bad. I had broken ribs and I was badly bruised, but I survived.

"We were kept in this barracks for the duration. We had some more burial details and had to cut some wood, but I never talked much after that."

Rations

"Every morning they would bring us a big container of coffee. It was hot water with a little color in it, sometimes more than others. Some guys used it to shave with. It really wasn't good to drink, but it was hot and I drank all they gave me. At noon they would give us a bowl or can of soup. All I had to eat out of was a tin can I got out of the garbage. I had whittled a spoon out of a piece of wood. At night they would give us a loaf of German black bread, which was divided between seven men. Each day a man would take turns cutting the bread. The guy that did the cutting got the last draw. Each day someone else took a turn. You also got the crumbs, but you had to be careful not to make too many crumbs or you would be accused of being too messy. It is humorous now, but it was serious then. I weighed about 160 when I was captured and at the end of 105 days, and that's after I had been eating good, I only weighed 94 pounds."

Liberation, April 2, 1945

Ken and the other prisoners in the camp were liberated on April 2, 1945. "There were a lot of Englishmen in the camp. Most of them were in bad shape. They wanted to be moved out of the camp first. By the fourth day we were still there, although we were eating pretty good. A medic came in one day and said, isn't anyone sick? We looked at him and said, isn't everyone sick? He told us if we wanted to get out of the camp before the English we better get sick. Before the day was over every American prisoner was sick. They moved us out by truck into an open field where they had showers set up.

"You could imagine how the body lice were in the place. We had longhandles on and part of the pastime was to pull your underwear off and turn them inside out and pop the big body lice. You could imagine the odor on them after a while. We went through the showers and took our underwear and burned them. Then they gave us new clothes. Then we were put on C-47s and sent to Camp Lucky Strike in France."

Camp Lucky Strike

Ken and his fellow prisoners arrived at Camp Lucky Strike looking forward to good food and lots of rest. However, their stay started with a tragedy. "The first day that we were there a fellow that I knew by the name of Warren went by a Red Cross set up for coffee and donuts. He didn't know when to quit. The donuts ruptured his stomach and he died. After all that he had gone through, to die over a donut."

After about ten days of medical checks, good food, and rest, Ken was heading home.

Homeward Bound, April 22, 1945

On April 22 Ken boarded the USS *Argentina* and headed for the United States. Thirteen days later on May 5, 1945, the ship landed at New York Harbor. The only people to greet them as they went down the plank were Red Cross ladies with boxes of ice cream.

"We went to Camp Kilmore, New Jersey, and de-programmed. We were supposed to forget all about what happened to us. Then they give us partial pay and 60 days' furlough. Why they did that, I don't know. There wasn't a man in the outfit that was physically fit to go on furlough. I look back on it now and I wasn't ready to meet my family. I got on a train and went to South Chicago and met my sister. We went out to the house and they had a big party planned for me. I had worked in Chicago and had a lot of friends there. We had a party and I drank a lot of whiskey and it almost killed me. Everyone wanted to talk, but all I wanted to do was put it behind me.

"Two days later I came home. Mary, my girlfriend, was waiting on the curb for me. We had planned on getting married if I made it back. Two weeks later, on May 20, 1945, we were married."

Fifty Years Later

Ken didn't attend a veterans' association meeting until 1988. He had a great time and after that became more active in veterans' associations. Then an amazing thing happened. Some German soldiers who fought in the Battle of the Bulge contacted the editor of the 106th Association magazine. They wanted to have a reunion with some of the soldiers of the 106th Division. In September 1995, 16 veterans returned to the battlefields in Belgium. Ken was one of those veterans. "We had a great time. I got rid of a lot of ghosts. We were going down the road and weren't sure where we were. I looked up and I said I have been in that house. One of the guys looked up and said, you got to be crazy. I said no and he stopped. It was the house we had gone in 50 years ago. I went to the house and a young lady answered the door. I went in and it was just like it was that day we had been in it. I couldn't believe it.

"I took a photo at the point where I was beaten by a German soldier. We walked the route and reminisced with the soldiers that were once our enemy. The war was history and the fact that we were once enemies was history also. By the end of the reunion there was a bond among us. No one said it, but we could all see it in each other's faces."

POINTS OF INTEREST

Battle of the Bulge Facts

1. During the Battle of the Bulge, from December 16, 1944, to January 25, 1945, the weather was the coldest within memory in the Ardennes Forest area.
2. The 106th Infantry Division alone suffered 416 killed in action,

1,246 wounded and 7,001 missing at the end of the offensive. Most of these casualties occurred within the first three days of battle, when two of the division's three regiments were forced to surrender.

3. The surrendering of 7,001 men of the 106th Infantry Division was the largest single recapitulation since Bataan.

4. At Malmedy, 86 American prisoners were lined up in a field and murdered by SS troops. The Malmedy Massacre was the worst atrocity committed against American troops during the course of the war in Europe.

5. In its entirety, the Battle of the Bulge was one of the worst battles in terms of losses to the American forces in World War II.

Nazi Concentration Camps

Many Americans taken prisoner of war during the Battle of the Bulge were sent to Nazi death camps: Stalag IXA near Zigenheim, IXB near Bad Orb, and IXC at Berga and Elster. The largest single group were members of the 106th and 28th Infantry Division.

On Christmas day, 1944, the first of 800 men arrived in boxcars at Stalag IXB. The Germans separated the Jewish-American soldiers at Stalag IXB and moved them with many non–Jewish soldiers to Stalag IXC in Eastern Germany, which was part of the Buchenwald death camp. The Americans were put to work 14 hours a day drilling a tunnel for a rail line. Guarded by the SS, many were beaten to death and few returned home.

SERGEANT CHARLES BRANUM
U.S. ARMY

71st Infantry, 5th Interceptor Combat Unit
Captured During the Fall of Bataan
Prisoner of War
April 9, 1942–September 15, 1945
Bataan Death March, Camp O'Donald,
Bilibid and Mukashima

A Volunteer to the Philippines, 1939

After quitting college in 1939, Charles Branum volunteered for the Army. He completed his basic training and then received orders to the Philippine Islands. There Charles was assigned to the 2nd Observation Battalion Squadron in Manila. His unit was moved a short time later to Clark Air Force Base. Charles had regretted quitting college and wanted to better himself. He excelled at his duties as an enlisted soldier and strived to become a good leader. The drive and determination landed Charles a spot in a class of candidates with the West Point preparatory school. He once again excelled and looked forward to becoming an officer, but it was not to be. Before could finish officer training, the war broke out.

The Japanese Attack, December 8, 1941

The Japanese attacked Pearl Harbor on December 7, 1941, and destroyed the U.S. Pacific Fleet. Their strategy was to isolate the Southeast Asia area from any help from the United States. On December 8,

1941, the Japanese began a series of bombing raids throughout the area, including the Philippine Islands. After 14 air raids the Philippine and American air forces were all but totally destroyed. Two days later, the Japanese made a land invasion at Aparri, Virgan, and the Bataan peninsula in the Philippines. There they would make their last stands.

The battle of Bataan began on January 9, 1942. The allies were subjected to endless bombardment by Japanese artillery and air power. They attacked in full force. In spite of the overwhelming superiority in numbers, arms, equipment and disputed air power, the defenders held their positions, often in hand-to-hand combat with the enemy.

The attack by the Japanese had become so costly that General Homma seriously thought about abandoning the attack on the Philippine Islands and bypassing the islands in order to meet the schedule of conquering Southeast Asia. One more attack, however, was in favor of the Japanese. They made an attack with 50,000 soldiers supported by 150 artillery guns on the line of defense that had been weakened by starving conditions and disease. The assault lasted for four days, ending with the surrender on April 9, 1942, of 76,000 Filipino and American troops.

Following the surrender of Bataan, the Japanese immediately began bombardment of Corregidor, an island in the entrance of Manila Bay. Bombardments continued every day until May 5, 1942. The last day of bombardment destroyed everything on Corregidor — communications, guns, supplies, and even the morale of the defenders. The following day, Corregidor fell into the hands of the enemy.

From the first day of the bombing, Charles was involved as a defender, first on Corregidor, then on Bataan. He performed bravely and would later receive six Purple Hearts, two Silver Stars, and one Bronze Star for his performance: but not before he would go through the pure hell of the Bataan Death March and 1,232 days as a prisoner of war under the Japanese Imperial Army.

Charles' Story, December 8, 1941–April 17, 1942

"The first place they bombed was our school in Baguio. Seventeen bombers came over and we thought they were ours. We went to the windows to look at them and after we looked for a minute we realized they weren't our planes — bombs fell everywhere. They kept making passes all day and tore up the town of Baguio and our base, Camp Hay.

"After days of continuous bombing, we had to evacuate on Christmas day 1941. We went across headhunter territory. As we traveled, we got acquainted with these headhunters and they agreed to get a Japanese head every chance they got. We got across the mountains and two of us were assigned to a lookout post. The rest of the group headed for this little town, took a bus, and headed for Manila.

"The two of us were on the outpost and we could see that the Japs were bombing this little town. The group that went ahead of us had sent a bus for us and when we boarded the bus we told the driver we wanted to go through this town. He didn't want to take us, but we made him. What we didn't know was the Japs had taken the town. He knew it, but we wouldn't listen. When we got to the edge of town, we saw Japs everywhere. It was dusk and they were camping around the area cooking meals. We told the driver to take his time and go on through the town as if nothing was wrong. We leaned back and he drove right through the whole group of Japs. We were so close we could have touched them. They never saw us because we leaned back so they couldn't tell who we were. We made it through and finally reached our troops."

Corregidor

"I couldn't find my unit and I had some training with machine guns so this lieutenant assigned me to one of the guns. We continued on and came to where the defenders were camping out. The lieutenant in charge of us came from Corregidor and needed to return. Since I couldn't find my outfit, he wanted me to go with him. We were able to get to a water barge and made it to Corregidor and I stayed there for about three or four weeks. The Japs were bombing the place continuously.

"Some of the troops had made a bomb shelter by digging a big hole and placing jungle leaves over it. There were steps going down into the shelter. It looked unsafe to me. One day I was eating breakfast and the Japs came over. We headed for the shelter. I told the cooks as we started in that I wasn't going down in the hole. I didn't trust it. I stayed on the

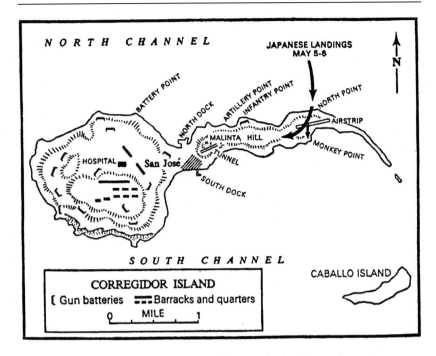

NORTH CHANNEL

JAPANESE LANDINGS
MAY 5-6

N

BATTERY POINT

NORTH DOCK

ARTILLERY POINT
INFANTRY POINT

NORTH POINT

AIRSTRIP

HOSPITAL   San José

MALINTA HILL

TUNNEL

MONKEY POINT

SOUTH DOCK

SOUTH CHANNEL

CABALLO ISLAND

CORREGIDOR ISLAND
[Gun batteries ▀▀▀ Barracks and quarters

0   MILE   1

Map of Corregidor Island (Sgt. Charles Branum).

steps and it was a good thing. A bomb hit near the shelter; it caved in and killed forty men. I didn't find that out for a while because I was hit on the back of the head and I was out for hours. I was lucky, though, because I stayed on the stairway and avoided the cave-in."

Battle of the Points: Bataan

"When I woke up, I found some wounded men and helped them down to the hospital. Some were kept in the hospital, but I was released. I decided that I should go back to my unit on Bataan. So I returned to Bataan, but never could find my outfit. I was put in the provisional infantry, the 71st Infantry, 5th Interceptor Combat Unit. They were good men and they taught me a lot. There were points that the Japs would land on and we would form a line to hold them back. They were trying to get to this road that went around the peninsula. We fought on a point called Aglaloma. I was wounded several times but not too seriously.

"Then we moved to a second point and I was wounded in the chest area. We finally had a main line across Bataan, but we were assigned to the battle of the points. One night the Japs made a night landing. I was looking through a scope and spotted them coming in. I called in artillery and we were hitting them with 155 rounds. Then I moved back up to my machine gun and myself and the other machine gunners emptied 250 belts of ammo into the landing boats. Finally, our P-40s came in and started bombing them. We were doing really well until some of the P-40s mistook us for Japs and started firing on us. Another big problem we had was the disease. More than half of us had malaria, beri beri, or dysentery if not all of them. It was a day to day dog fight, but we were able to move them back off the points at least temporarily."

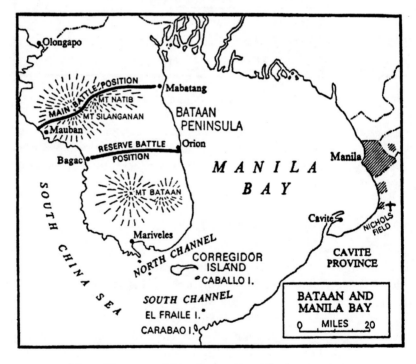

Map of Bataan and Manila Bay (Sgt. Charles Branum).

Surrender, April 9, 1942

"After we ran all the Japs off this point, we were assigned to another point. Then we moved to a point near Corregidor. All of the points had been taken back from the Japs when they made their final assault. They had thousands of troops and by now we had the weakest line of defense that we had since the battle started. The battle lasted four days and was then followed by three days of bombing. Then we got word on the telephone to surrender. We had wire strung all over the jungle to contact each other and sometimes a Jap would be on there. Some could speak good English and they would try to trick us. When I picked up the phone and they told us to surrender, I told them to go to hell because I thought it was a Jap. We found out later we really were supposed to surrender. It was a horrible night.

"We were told that if we saved our trucks they would move us in them. We lined our trucks up on the air base. It was a horrible feeling because we didn't know what they would do to us. We had heard that they didn't take prisoners. When they came in, they didn't seem to bother us at first, but they didn't use the trucks. We had to walk. The walk later became known as the Bataan Death March."

Bataan Death March,
April 9, 1942–April 17, 1942

"I was walking by myself and there were no guards around. I could have escaped into the jungle, but there was no place to go. We continued to walk and they began to separate us into groups. Then we had to stay together. I was on the march for nine days. I had to walk about 90 miles. I helped two men that were in my unit. I was healthy and they weren't in good shape because of the wounds they had received while we were fighting the Japs. The march itself is hard to describe. I don't know the words to use, but it was horrible. They were killing men every few minutes. You would hear a gun go off and a short time later we would walk by a dead soldier.

"We had stopped for a short time and then the Japs told us to move out. The guy beside me staggered as we stood up and a Jap shot him in the arm. He spun and fell down. This Jap went over and put his foot on the other arm, pinning him down, and bayoneted him in the chest. He hadn't done anything, just staggered. We had to leave him right there.

"They inspected us every mile. They would make us lay everything down on the ground in front of us. I didn't have anything because I had lost it all, but they found one guy with razor blades which he had with his shaving equipment. They told us that they were going to kill ten men plus the man that had the razor blades. They started picking men out and the guy next to me was picked when we stopped. They took the men in front of us and made us line up and they shot them right in front of us. They just left them on the trail.

"All along the trail as we walked, you could see dead Americans and Filipinos lying beside the roadside. After we got out of the mountains into the lowlands there were all kinds of artesian wells, but the Japs still wouldn't

The Bataan Death March (National Archives, Washington, D.C.).

Prisoners on the Bataan Death March (National Archives, Washington, D.C.).

let us have any water. Some of the men were so thirsty they broke and ran for the wells to get a drink and the Japs shot them all. There were about 20 men and they killed every one of them just because they wanted to get a drink of water.

"The next day the Jap guard let us go to a well and fill our canteens and then drink all the water we wanted. It was on the last day of the march. It was nine days of hell."

Camp O'Donald

At the end of the march the prisoners were jammed into boxcars and taken to Camp O'Donald located at Capas, in north central Luzon. They were housed in nips (shacks) that had been formerly used by the Filipino Army. About 1,500 American prisoners died in this camp.

"After we got to Camp O'Donald the men were dying so fast from dysentery, starvation, and malaria that we had a hard time keeping up with burials. We had a place called Boot Hill where we buried the men in mass graves. A few days after we buried them, it came a hard rain and washed away much of the dirt. You could see arms and legs sticking up out of the ground.

"I volunteered to go on work details because I thought I might get something to eat. On occasion I did and I would bring part of the food back to these two wounded men I had been helping. I was on a work detail building a road. The Japs were trying to build a road from our location to the Philippine sea. There were 300 of us that went on the detail and in two weeks there were only about 50 of us left. I was covered with tropical ulcers and would have died if I had used this medicine that a buddy of mine had stolen from the Japs.

"I was lucky in a way that I got sick and was transferred out of the

Prisoners at Camp Donald, in a photo taken by Japanese to show the world they were treating prisoners well (National Archives, Washington, D.C.).

A photograph at Camp Donald staged by the Japanese to present an appearance of well-cared-for POWs (National Archives, Washington, D.C.).

prison camp because the Japs were so brutal there. When prisoners were brought in if the Japs found any Japanese money or tokens, the prisoners were immediately beheaded. Prisoners were marched without food or water, made to sit out in the sun without any protective cover, continually beaten, and couldn't lie down at night.

"Prisoners too weak to work or march were killed. On one occasion I saw three Americans buried alive. One officer was trying to help another soldier and he was beaten until he passed out. These people were inhuman."

Bilibid Prison Camp

The Bilibid prisoner of war camp was located in the heart of Manila. The camp was designed by the Americans during their occupation of the islands as a place of detention for Filipino criminals before World War II.

The camp consisted of approximately 11 long one-story buildings, one large main building formerly used as a hospital, and one at the end of the grounds, a two-story administration building constructed partly of wood and partly of concrete. The prison grounds were laid out in the form of a wheel with a stone wall surrounding the grounds and forming the rim. The long, low buildings were the spokes. The wall had three entrances and guard towers were located at several places along the wall.

Prisoners of the Japanese were strip-searched as they arrived at the camp and were allowed to keep one uniform, a shelter half, and a blanket. A poor quality rice diet with an occasional rotten vegetable was all the food prisoners were allowed. Outbreaks of dysentery, beri beri, and malaria were common. The Japanese beat prisoners for the smallest infraction or for no infraction at all.

Charles was transported by truck to Bilibid along with 50 other prisoners. Nine of the prisoners died on the way. Charles arrived at the prison covered with tropical ulcers. The Japanese had captured a medical naval unit and they treated Charles. The medical team finally got the sores under control. The Red Cross had sent food parcels to the camp and Charles was allowed to split one with another prisoner. Charles stayed in this prison camp until he got well enough to work. From that point on Charles was assigned to a series of work details that would last until late 1943.

"We were sent out to work on Nielson Field making a concrete runway for the Japs. I spent Christmas day 1942 working on the field. We were on a straight rice diet. The rice was full of worms. They were white with black heads. They laid eggs in the rice and it often had webs in it. You would have to eat the worms and pick the webs off like cotton candy. We began to go blind because of a vitamin deficiency. Everything was a blur. The American doctors didn't know if we would ever get our eyesight back, but as we got used to the food we began to get better. We only got water to drink.

"After we completed the air strip at Nielson we were moved to a Filipino army air base. It was really hard work on this field. We hauled rock for another air strip. They would dynamite the rock and it would come down in big rocks. Then we would have to break up the rock with picks. The whole time we worked the Japs would beat us. They would beat us for not working fast enough or really for no reason at all. Several men were beat to death with pick handles. If you had any gold in your teeth, they would knock your teeth out to get the gold.

"One day I was carrying rock, this Jap came and got me. He took me to the guard house where there were eight Jap guards. They grabbed my shorts and pulled them off. Then each one of them would take turns putting cigarettes out on my back and testicles. Each time one would do it they all burst out laughing. When they finished their little game, they beat me with a bamboo club and sent me back out to the rock pile. My testicles began to swell and I was sick for several days from the incident. I had to keep working though.

"One day they were going to set some dynamite and the Americans were putting the dynamite in the holes the Japs had drilled. I was working near a rock edge and I didn't notice this guard go over and put wires on the generator and set the dynamite. Two Americans who had been set-

Prisoners secretly celebrate the 4th of July in a Japanese prison camp. Had they been caught they might well have been killed (National Archives, Washington, D.C.).

ting the dynamite were killed and the rock that I was on slid down and I slid with it. A heavy rock landed on my left foot. There were no broken bones, but my foot was smashed really bad.

"After I got hurt, they put me to work in the kitchen. The Japs would go into town to get the food and would get some tobacco for the prisoners to smoke if they wanted. I didn't smoke. They were allowed to get a bushel basket of fish to feed six hundred men. All we could do is to make a soup out of it and pour it over the rice. There were days when all they did was to provide us with shell corn to eat. We had to cook that and the skin wouldn't come off and it was hard to eat. All you could do was swallow it and we didn't have anything to go with it."

Hell Ship to Japan

In the latter part of 1943 Charles was selected along with a hundred other prisoners to go to Japan. They walked to the docks and boarded a hell ship for Japan. Charles never did know the name of the ship because it was an old rusty freighter and there was no name on it. He simply called it a Hell Ship, and rightfully so. "They put 1,000 of us on this old rusty freighter. We didn't have any place at all to lie down. It was so hot in there you couldn't get your breath. Several guys suffocated on the trip. They wrapped them in canvas and they were dumped overboard. I got lucky again because they needed 20 cooks. I never dreamed that my name would be called, but mine was the 19th name called. I stepped out of that hole and got some fresh air. It was wonderful. Twenty of us getting out of the hole helped for more room for those in the hole, but 20 plus the men that died, about 15 or 20 at the time, wasn't much out of 1,000.

"I was on top because of being a cook and I watched as we moved across the ocean. We were in a convoy with other freighters. We didn't know if the other ships had prisoners on them or not. On the way to Japan one of the submarines hit and sunk one of the ships in our convoy. We were lucky we weren't hit."

"We made it to Kobe, Japan, several days later on my birthday, September 4, 1944. I was 24 years old. It was a good birthday present to get off of that hell ship. We were put on a train. They made us pull the shades down over the windows. We went north for about three hours. Then they took us off the train and put us on a ferry and took us to the island of Honshu."

Camp Mukaishima, September 1944–September 1945

On the island of Honshu, bordering a small inland sea about 30 miles due east of Hiroshima, were eight camps in the Hiroshima group. Camp Mukaishima had barracks divided into three rooms for the prisoners and was approximately 30 feet by 130 feet. The barracks contained double deck sleeping platforms.

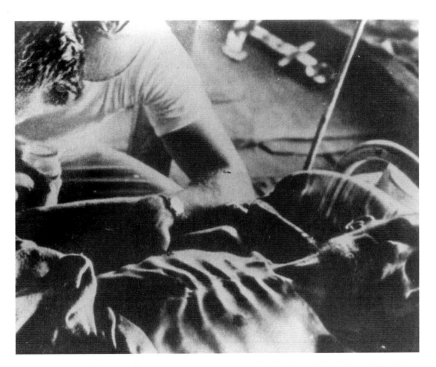

POW at a Japanese camp in the Philippines, 1943 (National Archives, Washington, D.C.).

The buildings were constructed of rough wood, unpainted inside and out. The roof was made of fireproof paper. The floors were rough wood. There was no heat. The latrines were wooden boxes with six holes covering a concrete pit which had to be emptied every week. The urinal was on the partition that separated the last sleeping room from the latrine. There were six spigots to wash from, but the water was not drinkable.

This prison camp was by far the best that Charles had been in. The food consisted of rice and steamed barley, and although there was never enough, it was much better than what he had in the past. Luckily so, because Charles had dropped from a muscular build of 165 pounds down to a frail 85 pounds. "There was a dock yard there that repaired ships that had been damaged. I was made an electric welder and I welded plates to patch the holes in the ships. We stayed in this camp for the rest of the war. There was a British camp across the road from us and they had built barracks for us on the opposite side. We worked with the British and they taught us a lot about welding. It was really easy work. All we did was weld, nothing else.

"It was a lot better camp than we had been in. It was cold and we had to put up with that, and many of the British prisoners had died from the weather in the years prior to our arriving, but we made it. We got to take a bath once a week. We had a big wooden tub over on the British side. We would heat the water and would have to use small buckets to wash with. We got soap and it was the first I had since being a prisoner. The last ones to use the tub got to get in the tub and it was a pleasure being in the water.

"B-29s started bombing Japan daily. They would take us to the mountainside and make us get in sandy caves. They were dangerous to be in, especially if the bombs hit near by, but we never had to worry about it because they never came close.

"What did worry us were the Japs, because we knew the war was getting close to the end. The Japs thought we were going to make an invasion on land. They had signs up all over the place with orders to kill every POW when the first American set foot on Japan. Kill them by any means. No one was to escape. We were all afraid we were going to be killed because there was no place to escape."

The A-Bomb, August 6, 1945

"We went to work at the dock yard as usual on the morning of August 6. I was on the mast of a ship that was in dry dock. I saw the plane go over. It had been doing this for several days. This day it flew over us and all of a sudden there was a big flash. At first I thought I had struck an arc with the welder. Then there was a huge mushroom cloud forming in the sky. There was a mountain range between us and Hiroshima. We watched the cloud until we could feel some of the shock waves. It blew some windows out of a few buildings. We didn't know what it was; we thought a bomb had hit an oil well. The mushroom cloud got higher. It was scary, an uneasy feeling, but we still didn't know what it was.

"Around noon that day I got caught with some food I had stolen. The Japs beat me and slapped me around all afternoon. Then they took us back to the camp. They told us that there would be no more beatings or kneeling on the concrete. We weren't sure what had happened yet, but we knew it was something big.

"The A-bomb dropped about nine miles from us and we did get radiation. We just didn't know it. None of us in the camp had any problems, but there were twenty men in Hiroshima when the bomb hit. They brought two of them in our camp and one of them had mucus running out of his eyes, nose, and ears. Shortly after that the Japs removed some of the more odious guards from the prison camp.

"Then when the bomb was dropped three days later in Nagasaki we saw a big change in the Japanese. They were always bragging about what they had done to us, but this day they wouldn't even look at us. They just walked around with their heads bowed. We knew the war was over, but the Japs wouldn't tell us anything. Finally, we were told to go over to the British side. They had stolen a radio and we heard that we were supposed to listen for a message from [General Douglas] MacArthur. He told us that the Japanese had surrendered on August 14, 1945. He told us to stay in the compounds, but he might as well have said to get out of them and go where you want to, because that's what we did."

The First American Flag Over Japan, August 18, 1945

The POWs had a month wait before they were liberated. The prisoners had lowered the Japanese flag of the rising sun and realized that they didn't have a flag to raise. American planes were dropping food by red, white and blue parachutes. The prisoners took the material to a local Japanese tailor shop to sew the flag. The Japanese worked constantly to finish the flag as soon as possible. On the morning of August 18, 1945, at 11:00 A.M., 99 of the surviving prisoners fell out for a formal flag-raising ceremony. "I was selected to raise the flag. One of the men took a bugle off an abandoned Jap cruiser and played 'To The Colors' while I raised the flag with tear filled eyes."

Liberation, September 15, 1945

For the next month the prisoners raised the flag with a formal ceremony each morning, then spent their time eating and enjoying the freedom of movement for the first time in three and one half years. Millions of yen were left everywhere. Charles picked some up and put them in his billfold as souvenirs because he didn't think they were any good. To his surprise, when they were liberated he found out that he could turn it in for money. He had left a barracks full.

On September 15, 1945, the men lined up and marched to the port of Onomichi, where they were officially liberated. On this march to freedom the homemade flag was carried and displayed before the liberated prisoners.

Charles and his fellow prisoners caught a plane and landed in Okinawa. "We were getting ready to leave there and we had to go to sick call. I didn't want to because I knew that I was sick. Well sure enough, I had fever and they put me in the hospital. This major that made me go to sick call walked nine miles to this hospital just to tell me that he and the other men that I had been with had to leave. While I was there everybody wanted to come to the hospital and look at me because I was the first POW in there. I was moved up into the mountains to another location with fewer men. We had a movie one night and were hit by a Jap that held up in the mountains. He sprayed the area with an automatic weapon. No one was hurt, but I thought that all this was over with."

Home

"I got home to Sikeston, Missouri, in November 1945. My parents met me and hugged me. We drove home. We went down the country road and turned into the road that led to the house. I remembered every inch of that dirt road and how I played on it when I was a boy as we drove closer to home. When we got there, I couldn't believe I was home. After all those years I was home again."

POINTS OF INTEREST

Bataan Death March

Americans and Filipinos were herded together, and regardless of their condition, marched to San Fernando, a distance of about 140 miles. The march lasted for more than a week. Many of the men were forced to march without shoes or covering for their heads.

They were fed only twice during the march and were never given water. No one was permitted to lag behind. Anyone who fell behind or was caught trying to get food or water was either beaten, bayoneted, or shot.

The death march claimed the lives of 16,950 American and Filipino prisoners.

Camp O'Donald

From April 10, 1942, to May 5, 1942 (six weeks), nearly 1,600 American prisoners and 26,768 Filipinos died from lack of quinine and food, even though the Japanese army had plenty of food and medicine on hand.

TECHNICAL SERGEANT
GORDON K. BUTTS
U.S. ARMY AIR FORCE

451st Bomb Group (H), 725 Bomb Squadron,
15th Air Force
Shot Down Over Mostar, Yugoslavia,
During an Air Raid
Prisoner of War
April 17, 1944–May 7, 1945
Stalag Luft III, Stalag VIIA, and Stalag XIIID

Pre-War Enlistment, October 29, 1940

Gordon Butts enlisted in the Army at South Bend, Indiana, on October 29, 1940. He was sent to Fort Benjamin Harrison in Indianapolis for his basic training. After his arrival by bus he received his first Army meal — a bologna sandwich and a glass of milk.

From Fort Benjamin Harrison Gordon was send to Maxwell Field in Montgomery, Alabama, where he was introduced to what would become commonplace — six man G.I. tents constructed with wooden floors and frames. He was also introduced to Southern style cooking. One morning at the mess hall Gordon covered his cream of wheat with sugar and milk. It was grits.

Gordon was stationed at a couple of bases before he embarked on a troop ship to several ports in Central America: he debarked at Rio Hata, Panama, to build a technical school to train aircraft mechanics and worked as a clerk in the inspection division at Albrook Field near Panama. The major turning point in Gordon's career came in October 1942. He heard about an air cadet examination that was being given and anyone could take the exam. A buddy told him he couldn't pass the exam because it was designed for college graduates. Gordon was a high school graduate with six months of business college. He took the exam anyway and passed by one point. Then after passing a battery of physical and physiological tests, he was on his way.

Gordon begin flight training at Harlington, Texas, and washed out of flight school. It was the low point in his career. He was given a choice of officer training in the infantry or corporal in the Army Air Corps. He chose the Air Corps. Gordon trained for the next couple of months before being assigned as a gunner on a B-24H and then left for Europe.

Heading for Europe, December 1943

In December 1943, the group started overseas. The ground support personnel of the group went by ship. Each individual aircraft was to fly by itself to Africa. Gordon's group flew to West Palm Beach, Florida, stayed a couple of days, then went to Puerto Rico. They landed on the south side of the island. The next day took them to Georgetown, British Guyana, and then they were in Belem, Brazil. The next day the unit went to Natal, Brazil, and all Gordon can remember is flying over jungle. They stayed three days in Natal and all he did most of the time was check over the aircraft.

The group took off in the early morning over the Atlantic headed for Dakar, Senegal, West Africa. The navigator gave the crew an ETA (estimated time of arrival) and he was within ten minutes of the time. They were ten minutes early, and glad to have made it over 2,000 miles of ocean. They had an extra rubber gasoline tank in the bomb bay, but had not had to use it.

When the airplane landed Gordon heard a loud noise; he thought something was wrong with the plane. It was the metal lattice runway they were landing on: metal pieces hooked together to provide a hard landing surface. Each piece was about twenty inches wide, about ten inches long. They were used in most of the fields the crews were to land on.

They stayed at Dakar until all their group was in Africa. One day while the crew was training, word came down that one of the planes had lost some engines. The plane was about five miles out from the base. "We watched for them and could see the plane coming in on one engine. The runway was cleared and it came straight in. We never thought the plane would make it, but it did."

Most planes had a picture and a name painted on it and the crew that brought the plane in on one engine was no exception. They named their plane *Three Feathers*. There was a whiskey named Feathers so the crew painted a young lady holding a bottle of Three Feather Whiskey.

One other time while they were at Dakar, Gordon found out that the president was in the area. "President [Franklin] Roosevelt returned from a meeting with [British Prime Minister Winston] Churchill and boarded a cruiser in the bay. I had binoculars and watched the president being put aboard. I didn't know he couldn't walk and was in a wheelchair. I didn't know because the news reporters always took photographs of him from the waist up and they never wrote about him being in a wheelchair."

As time went on Gordon's crew decided that they wanted a picture and name painted on their plane. "We met and chipped in $10.00 to get the job done. After several days of discussion among the crew the pilot finally decided we had discussed it enough and named the plane *Honey-chile*."

From Dakar Gordon's crew flew to Marrakech, Morocco. On the flight over the Atlas mountains the carburetors on a couple of the engines iced up. "We turned the deicers on and the engines quit missing just about the time that the wings started to ice up. When the wings ice up they lose their lift. The deicers on the wings, which are located on the leading edge of the wing and move in and out to crack the ice, were turned on and the ice was removed. It was a busy time for a while."

"On the early part of the trip we flew over the Sahara desert at about 100 feet, looking for a B-24 that was missing, but we saw nothing. Years later the plane was found and the story was in *Life* magazine. They found no bodies and the plane was in good shape. It had landed, but not crashed. Another mystery."

They stayed in Marrakech until an air field was captured in Italy and they could fly in. Marrakech had a population of over 100,000 and was a tourist vacation spot before the war with major hotels and many gambling casinos. "I saw my first French Foreign Legion soldier there. When they would enter a café, they would stop and salute, then enter. This was in case there were any officers in the café."

The city had two parts, a European section and a native section called Medina. The native section was off limits to G.I.s. "Being the good G.I. that I was, I wanted to see why we shouldn't go in. The native section was a walled city with large gates. The gates were closed at sundown. I went to the native part of the city and stayed too long. I was caught in the city when the gates were closed. What to do? I saw a moor pulling a cart loaded with hay. I stopped him and asked how much he would charge me to take me through the gate. We settled on $10.00 and he hid me under the hay. He took me through the gate without any trouble. The best ten dollars I had ever spent because I didn't want to lose my stripes."

In December of 1943, the crew moved to Italy. They landed in Gioia Del Colle, Italy. They had tents, open mess halls, tent showers, and a wash bench with cold water faucets.

The First Missions

"Our landing strip was again steel grating linked together. We flew a few practice missions and were ready for combat. Our first mission was on the coast of Fier Radar station on the coast of Albania. We were excited and a little afraid. We circled a few times trying to find the target. We had no flak and saw no fighters.

"Now we were combat wise, we thought — no fighters, no flak. Why? We missed the target by five miles and had dropped the bombs in an open field. Mission one was over and only 49 to go."

The next missions were at radar stations and a marshaling yard, then a mission to support troops. The *Honeychile* ran into flak but had very little trouble with fighters. Mission number six was to support the ground troops at Anzio, Italy. They had a lot of flak and a few fights, but they were not hit.

On mission number 10 they bombed a marshaling yard and then a Messerschmitt Aircraft Factory in Regenburg, Germany. This was the toughest mission for the crew up to that time. Gordon's group led the mission with 40 aircraft. They flew without fighter escort. They were attacked almost continuously by the Luftwaffe ME 109 aircraft (German Air Force) and there was intense anti-craft flak from batteries near the target. During the aerial battle their gunners shot down 16 ME 109 fighters, but lost six B-24s.

"I shot down my first ME 109 on this mission. The 109 tried to fly up and through the formation. I was manning the top turret. When I saw him he was about 150 feet from us. I could see the pilot in the cockpit clearly. I fired. Other planes in the formation saw the plane explode. You had to have verification from other crews to claim a kill.

"We were so beat up after landing at Foggia Air Field in Italy, about 50 miles from our home base, that night I couldn't sleep. All I could think about was the pilot's mother. War is hell.

"I had another experience with 109s later. We were on a mission and there must have been a squadron of them. In your turret you have two .50-caliber machine guns. In order to charge [load] the round into the barrel, you pull a cable with a handle on it, then let go. This puts a load into the chamber and you are ready to fire. My left gun jammed and would not fire. The right gun quit firing. I tried to charge the right gun and the cable broke. Each gun had a sear pin. It is a safety device; the end of the pin sticks out about three quarters of an inch. I reached down and got a spent casing and stuck it into the sear pin and pulled. I was able to charge the gun so it would fire; I continued to fire one gun for the rest of the fight. When we landed I tried with one hand then with both hands to charge the gun. No luck. This shows what you can do when adrenaline kicks in during a fight."

On the next mission Gordon's crew hit Foulon Sub Pens in France, then a marshaling yard in Northern Italy. The yards were in a valley and the sky was black with flak bursts. They received some flak damage, but nothing serious.

On the next mission, on March 15, 1944, they bombed the city of Cassino, Italy. The German ground troops used an old church ruins to dig in. Only part of the group dropped bombs because of cloud cover. This turned out to be a difficult time. "We were over the target and I was told to go to the back of the plane. The bombardier had opened the bomb bay doors. Since I had to walk on the catwalk I closed them. I just got in the back of the plane and the bombardier let the bombs go. The bomb bay doors were closed and the bombs took the door with them. I still had to walk back to the cockpit and my turret. All I could see was the open space and the ground below.

"As flight engineer you never wore a parachute, just a chest parachute harness. If you wore a parachute you could not get around inside the plane. I hung on to the bomb racks and walked the catwalk back to the cockpit. I thought I would catch hell when I got back to base, but no one said a word about the doors. The next morning we had a set of new bomb bay doors and were ready to go again."

From March 7 to April 4 of 1944 the crew flew missions about every day, unless they were grounded for repairs. They bombed a variety of targets in Rumania, Austria, Italy, and Hungary.

The morning of April 5, 1944, they found the target was to be Ploesti Oil Refineries in Rumania. This was the most heavily defended target in Europe. This refinery provided the greatest source of fuel for the German war machine in Europe. The Germans were determined to protect it and keep it operating. The last raid on Ploesti had been in August 1943. The mission was to go in at ground level. General Lewis H. Brereton, the commander of the mission, told the plane crews that they expected 50 percent loss of planes. The crews were not happy.

The losses were not quite that high. Of the 177 planes that went in, 54 failed to return. "The Air Corps felt if only 5 per cent of the planes were lost on a raid, it was a successful mission. The catch was that you had to fly 50 missions before you could go home. Fifty missions at the 5 percent rate is 250 percent, what chance did you have of going home?

"What actually happened in my squadron, the 725th, was that one full crew of ten and four other crew members from other crews got home. Of course, what keeps you going is that it is going to happen to the other crew, not you. We lived in a tent city separate from the ground maintenance and other personnel. In April every crew around us had been shot down. We were jittery.

"The next mission was going to be the big one, Ploesti.

"We all knew what had happened on the last raid. This was the group's 24th mission and our 20th. Only 30 more to go. The only thing that we felt good about was we were going in at 20,000 feet and we felt we had a chance. This was a major effort; several groups from Italy would be bombing the target from different directions. We expected a rough fight and it happened. We encountered many ME 109 fighters on the way to the target and more fighters as we came off the target. While over the target we received major flak. We received flak damage, but it could have been worse. I shot down two ME 109s on the raid, one going into the target and one coming off the target.

"We lost four B-24s over the target. For this raid we received a second Presidential Citation. One of the things most people don't realize is the ways the German air force attempted to shoot us down. We were bombed while in flight from German aircraft dropping bombs into our formation from above. This was not very effective. We did fear having ME 109s around with rockets trying to hit us. I only saw two bombers hit the rockets; they exploded on contact. The Germans would flip in back of our formation, out of range of our .50-caliber machine guns, and lob rockets into the formation. This was scary, but again not very effective."

After the Ploesti raid the *Honeychile* made raids on marshaling yards in Yugoslavia and Rumania and an airdome in Hungary and Rumania. It was a busy time in April 1944, four targets in four days.

Mission 23 — The Last Bombing Raid, April 17, 1944

"Dawn, April 17, 1944, another raid. This one was to bomb the Belgrade Zemun in Airdome, Yugoslavia. This was the groups 29th mission and our 23rd.

"It was a normal mission to the target, some ME 109s on the way and some flak over the target. We were hit by flak. We had bombed at 20,000 feet and were letting down to about 14,000 feet over the Carot Mountains in Yugoslavia. The mountains were about 10,000 feet. Intelligence had not told us that the Germans had 88mm anti-aircraft guns on the top of the mountains. We were literally flying down their barrels. They opened up and we were hit. The first hit was on number three engine. This is the engine that has the main hydraulic pump which enabled the pilot to control the aircraft.

"At this time I am standing between the pilot and co-pilot. I saw the pilot go through the regular check off of all controls, no response, and the bail out order was given. I had my chest parachute harness on. I hooked on my chute, checked to make sure the two snaps were secure, and got down off the main flight deck to the deck below. That was the last thing I remember. I think the airplane exploded and blew me clear. The next thing I remember was floating in space with my parachute open. What made the chute open, I don't know. Maybe the explosion caused it. I may have had a reaction, for we often practiced bailing out, after a mission, when we landed and stopped rolling. It will always be a mystery why more didn't get out. There were four men in the tail of the plane; the tail gunner and back turret gunner bailed out. The last thing the two men remembered was the two waist gunners fighting over who would open the bottom escape hatch. I often wondered why they didn't go out the open waist windows. Of the ten men in the plane three bailed out, two of the four in the tail and one, myself, in the cockpit end of the plane. The rest went down with the plane."

The Capture

"On the way down I was machine gunned by a ME 109. The silk of my parachute was full of holes, but I wasn't hit. I landed in a tree and my feet were about three feet off the ground. A German soldier came over and pointed a Luger at me and said in broken English, 'For you the war is over.' S/Sgt. Sanborn and S/Sgt. Tittle were on the ground when I landed. We were all taken to a jail in Mostar."

The Journey to Prison Camp

"We were in jail in Mostar for three days. We were interrogated. We had been trained only to give name, rank, and serial number. That's what we did. After I was interrogated, the German captain told me more about our group than I knew. He knew our group by our crashed plane.

"When our group had flown about 15 missions one of the tail gunners bailed out over Germany. We were told later that he was interrogated. I would say he was a spy.

"We were taken to Sarajevo. There was a large German garrison there. In the jail we would watch the new German recruits learning to march and do the goose-step. Our jail was okay, food fair, but we couldn't bathe or wash our clothes. We had only our flight suits. At Sarajevo the three of us were put on a train with three guards. On the train we went through many towns and cities we had bombed. A grand tour at German expenses. The next step was Budapest, Rumania, we stayed there for a couple of days, and then to Vienna, Austria. Here we were held in the mess hall at an army camp. We slept on the floor. We had been given two German army blankets, one to sleep on and one to cover with."

Stalag Luft III

"Our next step was at a POW camp at Sagan — Stalag Luft III. The camp was situated in a pine wooded area out of the city of Sagan. It is in Northern Germany near the old Polish border. There were four compounds of American Army Air Corps prisoners, three of Royal Air Force officers, British, Australian, and Canadians. Each compound had 15 buildings. Ten were barrack or blocks each housing 80 to 110 men. The high rank officers had 2 to 4 men per room; normally there were 10 men to a room. The blocks were one story much like the barracks we had in the U.S. Beds were double decker bunks.

"When we entered camp the prisoners lined up on each side of the road looking for some of their old outfit. I found no one from my group. We were taken to the supply building and issued new clothes. The clothes had been sent from Switzerland where supplies had been stockpiled. The uniforms were enlisted men's uniforms, even though this was an officers' camp. They issued us one overcoat, one pair of gloves, one pair of wool trousers, one belt, one G.I. blanket, two German blankets, one blouse, two pairs of winter underwear, one sweater, one cap, two wool shirts, two pair of socks, one pair of high top shoes, and four handkerchiefs.

"I was assigned to the enlisted men's room in a block. All the men were sergeants. They were expected to take care of the block. Officers could not work. This was the reason the camp had to have some enlisted men.

"I was lucky to end up in an officers' camp. In the enlisted men's Stalag the housing conditions were bad, and the food poor, not that ours was good. I was assigned to a room of ten men. Two men did the cooking, two men did the dishes and cleaned the rooms. Each man was responsible for his bunk and surrounding area. Sometimes duties were rotated. The rest of the men were assigned to block duty.

"After I had been there for a few days I was assigned to the compound's first aid room. I had had some Red Cross courses in first aid before joining the army. There were no doctors in the compound. In the center compound was a hospital manned by German, American, and British doctors for seven compounds of men. If we couldn't take care of a man we sent them to the compound hospital. There were three of us manning the first aid station. All new prisoners coming into the camp, if they were wounded or ill, were examined by us and if necessary sent to the hospital. The Germans furnished very few medical supplies. What supplies we had, we received from the Red Cross. In 1944, we received some much needed sulfur powder. We mixed this with iodine and this made a paste that we could put on wounds and cuts. It worked.

"Sanitation was poor. Bathing facilities were extremely limited. In theory the camp shower house could provide each man with a three minute shower weekly. If we got one a month, we were lucky, and it was cold water.

"I was housed in the west compound. Our American senior officer was Colonel Darr H. Alkire. His duties were to run the camp and he was our contact with the German Luftwaffe, who ran the camp. Again, we were lucky to be held by the Luftwaffe rather than the German Army.

"The camp was operated like a military base. We had appel [roll call] twice a day, morning and evening. In some cases there were special appel. An example would be when they wanted to search the blocks. There were guards stationed in gun towers armed with rifles and machine pistols. The guards were fourth class troops, either peasants or too old for combat duty or young men convalescing after long tours of duty or wounds received at the front.

"While we were in the camp we had no contact with other POWs. In addition to uniformed sentries, soldiers in fatigues hid under the blocks, listening to conversation in the block, looking for tunnels and making themselves generally obnoxious.

"Occasionally the Gestapo descended upon the camp for a long, thorough search. The only way we could get back at the guards was passive resistance at appel. Instead of falling in, we milled around, smoked, failed to stand at attention, and made it impossible for the Germans to take a count. This was not done often, for they would bring in regular German soldiers with rifles and machine guns. There was an escape committee operating in the compound, and men did escape. Any individual that wanted to try to escape had to have permission from the committee.

"The Germans did supply some hot food, about 1,900 calories per day. While this was insufficient, what they provided was mainly brown bread and potatoes, and meat three times a week, vegetables twice a week, and watered down soup on alternate days. To supplement the German food we received Red Cross parcels, most were American, some British and Canadian. This was food like we had at home and greatly appreciated. These parcels came out of Switzerland and were delivered to the compounds in G.I. Army trucks. These trucks were driven by Swiss civilians. We were to get one half parcel a week, but as the war went on the normal rations were a half a parcel every other week. Some of the items in the parcels were Spam, corned beef, salmon, cheese, dried nuts, crackers, Klim [powdered milk], orange powder, liver paste, and a chocolate bar. The chocolate bar became money; if we wanted to trade with anyone for something, the questions was how many bars of chocolate for the items.

"Each compound had an athletic field and volleyball court. POWs built a theater, the materials furnished by the Red Cross. Musical instruments were brought in by the Red Cross and several orchestra and choral groups were formed. There were bridge tournaments and a school was set up to teach a wide range of cultural and technical subjects by the former teachers. The Germans and the officers that ran the camp wanted to keep the men busy for morale purposes. Busy people don't cause trouble and try to escape.

"The sports equipment was provided by the Red Cross. There was a library, which is where I spent my time. I was lucky because I had a job at the first aid room. I worked six mornings a week and part of the afternoon. Some of the time I took patients to the hospital, which gave me a change of pace.

"Most of the prisoners were interested in keeping in shape. The most common exercise was to walk the compound circle. Starting from the outside guard fence, there were two more guard fences, which had coils of barbed wire between them. Then inside the prison was a space of about ten feet which was considered no man's land. If you were in this area you could be shot. Just in front of the no man's land was the walking path, which was about five feet wide, wide enough that three men could walk abreast. There were always people walking, except at night. At night we were locked in our block. If you went out of the block you would be shot.

"Walking the path was interesting because often you would find fresh dirt. This was a clue that someone was digging a tunnel. The tunnel diggers would carry the dirt from the tunnel in their pockets or small bags and dump it on the path. We would never ask about the dirt. Of course the Germans also watched the new dirt on the path, so the hunt would be on to find the tunnel. This was the camp from which the British soldiers attempted escapes in the film *The Wooden Horse*. They were caught as they came out of the tunnels and shot. The ashes were in urns in the Central Hospital, as a reminder not to try escape.

"In April, when I arrived, some of the blocks were planting gardens with seeds they got from home. Fresh vegetables would be a welcome to out diet. We did receive some mail from home and packages could be sent every three months. I received one package while I was at Sagan. My mother said she had sent three. These packages were often pilfered. We could send one letter a month; my mother did receive some letters. All mail was read and censored by the Germans. The International Red Cross made all the extras we received possible. We gave thanks to them.

"One day when we were walking the circle a German fighter flew low over the camp. It made a lot of noise, but no propellers. What made it fly? Then we realized this was the new jet fighter, the ME 262, the Germans were building. They started production too late to make a difference, thank God.

"There was always a friendly discussion between the fighter pilots and the bomber crews. It went like this: Fighter pilot, 'Your bomber crews shot me down. I was looking for protection, for I was having trouble; when I got in formation, you shot me down.' The answer, 'You pointed your nose at us; we had a standard rule, if any plane pointed his nose at us, we shot them down.' This discussion would go on for days.

"The reason for this discussion was that the Germans had rebuilt some of the American fighters from planes that crashed. They would come up and get into the formation and fly with us. Then all of a sudden they would kick their rudder and start firing. Whenever a fighter came into our formation we always trained our guns on them.

"Another reason I was glad I was in the officers' camp was because the guards were from the Luftwaffe, the German Air Force.

"We knew our troops were getting closer from the radio broadcast; mainly the BBC [the British Broadcasting Corporation] picked up on our canary. [The canary was an illegal radio in the American compound.] In a room next to the first aid station was a map of Europe. The map would show where the German battle lines were. On the same map the Americans would put on a line where BBC and the allies said the battle lines were. The Germans would come each day and look. They knew there was a radio in camp. They searched for it. Sometimes I think they didn't want to find it. The canary was never a topic of conversation in camp. It was understood you did not ask questions. Just enjoy the map. The lines were [put up with yarn and pins] that the Russian Army was not too far away.

"The big question was, would the Germans move us out before the Russians captured us?"

The March to Nuremberg, January 25, 1945

"We received the answer at 2100 hours [9 P.M.] on January 25, 1945. All compounds received German orders to move out on foot within 30 minutes. Colonel Alkire had told us two weeks before to be ready to move on a short notice. In knotted trousers used as packs and makeshift sleds, we packed clothing and all the food we had. The Germans issued one Red Cross parcel per man. We abandoned books, letters, camp records, and took our overcoat and blankets and left.

"By 2400 hours [midnight] all men, except some that couldn't walk, marched out into the bitter cold and snow in a column of threes. Destination unknown. Our guards from the camp went with us; they carried rifles and machine pistols. We marched all night, fifty minutes of marching and ten minute breaks, every hour. German rations consisted only of black bread and margarine obtained from the horse drawn wagon — the camp kitchen. Each compound marched separately, each could tell a different story.

"We slept in unheated barns, empty factories, and on the ground. After the first 24 hours we were given a thirty hour rest for recuperation. I am not sure where we were at this time or where we were going. The guards from the camp were old men and had trouble keeping up. The G.I.s told the guards that they would carry their rifles for them; they knew we couldn't escape in this kind of weather. At the first river we came to, we dumped all the rifles in the water. We had some very angry guards. We had a good laugh."

The Forty and Eights

"Later, we were loaded on unmarked 40-8 freight boxcars, 50 men to a car. They locked the doors. We were in the boxcars for three days and nights with no water and no sanitation. One corner of the car was reserved for a toilet area. But who could go in a corner with 49 men looking on. Our greatest fear was that our train would be strafed by our P-51s or P-47s. At that time of the war the fighter planes were sent out to shoot up trains or any other target of opportunity. The 40 by 8 meant forty men and eight horses. Fifty men in the car made it crowded. There were four boxcars of prisoners. And on the third day we changed trains at Nurnberg [Nuremberg].

"After being in the boxcars for three days we needed to relieve ourselves. Having no place to go, the guards kept us together in the marshaling yard; we looked at each other, took down our trousers, squatted down and let nature take its course. What a relief. Some picture, 200 prisoners getting relief."

Stalag XIIID

"Conditions at Stalag XIIID at Nurnberg were deplorable. The barracks had recently been inhabited by Italian POWs who left them filthy.

There was no room to exercise, no supplies, nothing to eat out of, and practically nothing to eat. The German rations were 300 grams of bread, 250 grams of potatoes, some dehydrated vegetables and margarine. A few days after our arrival, Red Cross Parcels started to arrive by truck.

"Toilet facilities during the day were satisfactory, the only night latrine was a can in each sleeping room. Many of the men now had diarrhea, the can had insufficient capacity, so the floors were soiled very soon. The barracks were not heated. The morale of the prisoners dropped to its lowest ebb."

The March to Stalag VIIA, April 3, 1945

"At 1700 hours [5 P.M.] on April 3, 1945, we were told to evacuate the Nurenberg camp and march to Stalag VII at Mooseberg. The Germans agreed that the Americans would take over the march. The Americans were responsible for preserving order, and that we would march only 20 kilometers a day, about 12 miles.

"On April 4, 1945, each POW received one food parcel and we started south. While we were marching through a marshaling yard near a highway, some P-47s dive bombed the yard. Two Americans and one British soldier were killed; three others were wounded. The next day a large replica of the American Air Corps insignia was placed on the road with an arrow pointing in the direction of the march. This ended the bombing of the column.

"Many of the men were very weak and had difficulty keeping up. This is when we started the flying wedge. The weaker prisoners were allowed to drift back through the column as we marched. Then a group of the stronger prisoners would take the weaker prisoners to the front of the column during the ten minute break. This was repeated every hour.

"Colonel Darr H. Alkire was now in charge of the column. He was an excellent officer and was responsible for many of the improved conditions during the march. The German guards were aware of how close the American Army was, and this helped. Even though the Americans were in charge the guards went with us. On the third day of this march diphtheria broke out among the prisoners. Since I was the medic, I did what I could, which wasn't much.

"A couple of days later I had the disease. I could hardly talk, my throat was beginning to close. We were camping near a barn. I climbed up into the hayloft. I thought I had had it and the hay was a soft place to lay. Later in the day I heard Colonel Alkire asking where Sergeant Butts was at. They told him in the hay loft. He shouted for me and wanted to know what the problem was. I crawled out to the opening and tried to answer. He couldn't understand me, but realized I had caught the diphtheria. He said to lie down and stay there.

"We had been getting Red Cross parcels on a regular basis, for we were near the Switzerland border. Since Colonel Alkire was in charge he told the German captain that we needed more Red Cross parcels, now. The German captain called Switzerland to send a truck load of parcels right away. The truck was there the next morning. They unloaded the parcels and told the driver to take me to the column ahead of us, for there was a doctor there. This was what the driver did. When he got to the column, they found the doctor. I had worked with him at Sagan. He asked what was wrong and when I tried to answer he knew. In his medical bag he had some diphtheria serum and he gave me 1,000 units and told the driver to take me to Stalag VIIA. It was down the road about 20 miles."

Stalag VIIA

"When I arrived at Mooseburg they put me in a barracks. This was where they dumped all the sick prisoners. There were no German or American doctors, no medical personnel at all. I don't remember much for the next few days. I had gone into a coma and just laid in my bunk. An Army corporal took care of me as I came out of the coma. He fed me, gave me water, and looked after me. I don't even know his name.

"The sanitation was unbelievable. When I was able to move I would crawl to the latrine. The latrine had a sloping floor, with holes in the floor. The holes took care of the human waste. There were no stools or sinks. When finished, I would crawl back to my bunk. I was very weak.

"This nameless corporal saved my life. This was near the end of April. General [George S.] Patton's 3rd Army and the Germans fought a battle with the camp in the middle. Bullets flew like mad in the barracks. A

View of Stalag VIIA, Mooseburg, Germany, which held the largest number of prisoners liberated at one time (National Archives).

British soldier in the bunk next to me was killed in his bunk by a stray bullet. It hit him in his mouth and came out the back of his head. We all talked and he told me he didn't want to go home. He had been captured in North Africa."

Liberation, May 7, 1945

"From the barracks we were taken to an evacuation field hospital for seven days. The rule was that after seven days you had to move up to another hospital. I was the last one to leave from my old barracks. At that time I was paralyzed in both legs, arms, throat, and I was down to 105 pounds.

"From the evaluation hospital we were flown out on a C-47 hospital plane. We were on the ramp waiting to get on the runway. The first plane took off, the second plane taxied to the runway, it tried to take off and crashed at the end of the runway. We taxied to the runway, and took off through the smoke of the crashed plane. I was afraid, because the last time I was in a plane it went down.

"They took me to a hospital in Reims, France, where I stayed for a few weeks. I began to get stronger. The next step was Camp Atterbury near Franklin, Indiana, at Wakeman General Hospital. At Wakeman I was given a lot of vitamins and all the food I could eat. I was a ramp [Released Allied Military Personnel] and treated very nicely. When I started to walk and could move around I went down to the recreation room to watch a ping-pong match. I noticed a young lady also in hospital clothing. I asked if the chair next to her was taken and she said no. This was the beginning of a lifelong experience. She was a WAC [Women's Army Corps] recovering from an appendix operation. We were married in the hospital chapel on September 7, 1945."

— 9 —

STAFF SERGEANT
EDWIN DOUGLASS, JR.
U.S. ARMY

Company F, 35th Division, 134th Infantry Regiment
Captured in Nancy, France
Prisoner of War
September 11, 1944–April 21, 1945
Stalag XIIA, IIIC, and IIIA

The Beginning, August 1942

America's involvement in World War II was eight months old in August 1942. Induction centers were full of young men being enlisted to fight the Axis powers. They came from the cities, small towns and rural farm areas all over the U.S. On August 17, 1942, Edwin Douglass, a farm boy from southern Illinois, received his induction notice. He was to report to the induction center at Scott Air Force base for entry into the Armed Forces. After a complete physical he was sent to Camp Wheeler, Georgia, for 13 weeks of basic training. Then he went to Camp Meade, Maryland for further infantry training.

It was getting close to Christmas and Ed wanted to go home. He was short of money. He explained, "It was during Christmas and we were drawing for six day leaves for Christmas. It was toward the end of the month when I drew mine and I was broke. I went to a buddy of mine that I had gone through training with. I told him that I was broke and I needed money to get home on. He asked me how much I needed and I told him I could make it on $20.00. I can still see him pull that money out of his

130

pocket. I thanked him and turned to walk off. He asked me if that was enough. Before I could go the furlough was canceled and I gave him his money back."

Right after Christmas they sent Ed's unit to California to train. He ended up in F Company of the 134th Infantry Regiment. But only after a mishap or two. (We were going through Texas on a train and we picked up a load of medics. We found out that we were supposed to go to the Quartermaster's Battalion, but they had a mix up. The medics went to the Quartermaster's Battalion and they sent the rest of us to the 134th Medics Battalion. We spent the night and the next morning were milling around when a T-4 came strolling through. He asked us how much medical training we had. We had this old sergeant that had been busted back at Camp Meade. He spoke up and said, 'Medical training hell! I wouldn't roll a pill for no son-of-a-bitch. I'm infantry!' After that they sent four or five of us at a time to different companies. That's how I ended up in F company."

F company was sent to Camp Roker, Alabama, to Tennessee for maneuvers, and then Camp Buckner, North Carolina. "That's where the rough training started. Two weeks in the Virginia mountains and then we boarded the USS *Eugene Anderson* for Europe. We ate twice a day and they had to feed twenty-four hours a day because they had too many people on the boat. It was crowded and we had to take baths in salt water. I was looking forward to seeing land soon."

The Landing in Europe, May 12, 1944–September 10, 1944

Ed's unit landed in Saint Ives, England, on May 12, 1944. For the next few weeks it rained daily. Then on July 5, 1944, the 134th Regiment landed on Omaha Beach, France. "We never even got our feet wet. Everything had been cleared for us during the D-Day invasion. Our first real big objective was Saint Lo, France."

The 134th hit Saint Lo on July 14, 1944. For the next 14 days the men took the town block by block, building by building, encountering snipers, machine gun and Nazi artillery and tank fire. Finally, Ed's unit seized the town on July 27.

After another 45 days of fierce fighting, the 134th regiment had taken Mortain, Montargis, and Troyes from the Nazis and on September 10, were on the outskirts of Nancy, France.

The Battle at Nancy, September 10, 1942

As the preparations were made to take the town of Nancy, France, orders were given to E Company, F Company, and part of G Company of the 2nd battalion to cross the bridge into Nancy. F Company started to move at 2200 hours. Although the unit took heavy casualties, within an hour the companies had raced across the bridge. It appeared that the strategy was working until the Nazis figured out what was going on.

The Nazis began to bring in heavy concentrations of artillery. Although the American units ordered tank destroyers and another platoon to the scene, they arrived too late and the Nazis counterattacked.

The 3rd Battalion was ordered down to cross the bridge. There were continuous flares, and endless mortar and artillery shells marked the bridge. The 3rd Battalion commander made his way toward the bridge in an attempt to locate the 2nd Battalion in a culvert beneath the approaches to the bridge. Medics were working on the wounded, soldiers worked vainly to keep the communications lines open, officers screamed into the telephones to make themselves heard above the bursting shells which were landing all around them. The intensity of the fire made it impossible to move, much less cross the bridge.

Then at 0130 hours on September 11, a tremendous explosion shook the ground. Ed and the men of the 2nd Battalion knew immediately that what they had feared most had just became reality. The bridge had been blown and they were cut off. Nazis screaming (Heil Hitler!) closed in. Now with their backs to the river, no communication, no visibility, and the presence of the German tanks, it was all too overwhelming. Ed was wounded, but the pain from the wound was nothing compared to the sick feeling in his stomach when he realized he could surrender or die. There was no other choice.

The Capture, September 11, 1944

"I think the Germans blew up the bridge," Ed said. "There were a lot of men that didn't get across the bridge, but those of us that did had to roll in on the bank of the river. The Germans were in front of us and they brought tanks in behind us. We were trapped. Orders came down to surrender. We threw our guns down and came out from behind the banks. We were lined up and we wanted to smoke. This German was standing out there with his gun and he pulled out his cigarettes and wanted to trade one of his for an American cigarette. I didn't really want to because I had tried one of the German cigarettes before and I didn't like them, but I traded with him anyway.

"A short time later they took me back to an aid station for a hip wound I had received. The Germans had a tent set up and they were bringing German soldiers in as well as us. They finally got around to taking the shrapnel out of my hip and we went to a small hospital somewhere around Nancy, France. We met this French orderly that had learned English from a book. He was really good at it and he came up one day and wanted to know what bullshit meant. He said that he could find bull and he could find shit, but he couldn't find bullshit. We told him it was slang."

Stalag XXIIA, Third Week of September 1944

Ed was in the hospital for about a week before they shipped him to Stalag XIIA. The camp was located just 600 yards from a marshaling yard in Lindberg, Germany. This transit camp fluctuated from 1,500 to 4,000 prisoners, depending on the time period of the war. The barracks were one story, approximately 40 by 130 feet, each containing ten rooms leading from a central hallway running lengthwise through the building. Most barracks had no furniture, but those that did had a small stove, a table, and a few stools. Bunks were stacked six high and each room, approximately 15 × 23 feet, was designed to provide for 16 men.

In the latter part of the war as the prison population increased, men were forced to sleep on the floor or ground, in some cases with nothing

The straw-strewn floor of a barn at Stalag XIIA, where hundreds of American POWs slept (National Archives, Washington, D.C.).

but straw for a bed. The bedding was louse infected and all the prisoners suffered with body lice. The roofs leaked, windows were broken, lighting was inadequate, and there was no heat. There was one cold water tap located in a building used for a latrine. The walls and stools in the latrine were covered with feces. The prisoners made fruitless efforts to keep the

The letters "P.O.W." on the roof of this barracks at Stalag XIIA protected the site from Allied air attacks (National Archives, Washington, D.C.).

area clean, but because all the prisoners suffered from dysentery it was impossible to control their bowels.

The food was inadequate. The diet was bread and soup. Most of the prisoners averaged 900 calories or less a day. "The Germans never mistreated us as far as beating us, but we didn't get much to eat. We got a Red Cross box that four of us had to share. It is what kept us alive. The packages had nine packs of Old Gold cigarettes in it and I got them all because the other guys that I shared with didn't smoke. Later I traded the cigarettes for food."

Ed was at Stalag XIIA for a few days and then he was packed onto a train with hundreds of other prisoners. He had no idea of his destination.

The Forty and Eight Boxcars, September 1944

The main transportation of American prisoners was by rail. The 40 and 8 boxcars were the most common. The 40 and 8 referred to by the

Germans meant forty men and eight horses. For the prisoners it was much worse. Prisoners were packed into the boxcars so tight that they were unable to sit or lie down. The cars were sectioned with men at both ends of the boxcar, separated in the middle of the car by barbed wire and an armed German guard. The floors of the cars were often covered with horse manure mixed with straw. When men could sit or lie down; but they had no choice but to lie in the manure. The men would travel for days without food or water. The trains would not stop between destinations and when they did most of the time the prisoners were not allowed off of the trains. Prisoners had to use one corner of the boxcar for relieving themselves. The conditions after days of traveling became deplorable.

Ed recalled, "We were in Stalag XIIA for a few days and then they loaded aboard the forty and eights to move us to another camp. We were packed in the train so tight that you couldn't roll over without the help of your buddies. We were fed bread once in the four or five days that we were traveling. No water.

"Several times we stopped in rail stations and the Germans would leave us on side rails with other detached rail cars. When our planes bombed they would leave us locked in. We saw a lot of damage, but were never hit.

"Many of us had relieved ourselves in one corner of the car. I was lucky, but many were not. They suffered from bad cases of diarrhea and could not control their bowels. As a result, many relieved themselves standing in place. The conditions were unsanitary and the smell became unbearable after a few days with the crowded conditions in the closed boxcar."

Stalag IIIC, October 1944–February 1945

After five days aboard the boxcars Ed and the other prisoners arrived at Stalag IIIC at Alt-drewitz in the northeast part of Germany. The camp was much like the other Nazi stalags. "I began to catch up with the guys that I had been captured with. There were six of us in the barracks. It was really getting cold and we did get a small ration of coal, but it wasn't enough. The barracks had double floors so we burnt the wood from one of the floors.

"We had a wash house with a water pipe that stuck up out of the ground. When it got cold the Russians got horse manure and packed around the pipe so that the pipe wouldn't freeze. It worked because we had water all winter. One latrine was an open pit behind the wash house.

"During Christmas 1944, they issued a Red Cross box that had boned turkey and the trimmings. Some of the boys saved potatoes out of their rations and we put on a good feed. It messed some of them up. They had so much rich food that I saw some of them sitting on the stool and throwing up at the same time. I didn't get sick, but I was lucky.

"A few days later one of the guys thought that he was over the diarrhea and stood up and let a fart. He shit all over himself. We all laughed, but it really wasn't funny.

"I walked outside after the feed and lit a cigarette. The old German guard was walking the post between the barracks. He was old enough to be my father. I had a full belly and was feeling pretty good, it being Christmas and all. He looked over at me and put his fingers up to his mouth. I took one of my cigarettes and lit it. I handed it to him and he carried on for an hour over that cigarette."

"A couple of months later the Russian front moved closer and closer. The Germans decided they would have to abandon the camp. The prisoners were on the move again."

The March to Stalag IIIA, February 1945

The Nazis picked about thirty of the prisoners, including Ed, and marched them into Alt-drewitz. "They put us in the basement of a house overnight. While we were there the Russians came into the town with tanks and shot the place up. The next morning the German soldiers were coming through picking up the dead soldiers, throwing them on the back of trucks and moving on. They made us help. We took a door off a house and used it as a stretcher. We would put a soldier on it and carry the body to the truck. This old German soldier on the truck would grab them by the hair of the head and pull them up on the truck and stack them. This German lieutenant came and got us and took us around the corner of this house to pick up a soldier. He was really shook up. He was shaking his pistol at us and spoke perfect English. He looked at us and said, 'Why in the hell did you Americans come over here and fight Germany? Why?' We never gave him any trouble because he would have shot us if we had.

"After that they marched us toward Stalag IIIA. There were a lot of refugees on the road. Most were Germans running from the Russians. We would stay in barns, houses, and basements on the way. On a couple of occasions we slept on the ground. We didn't get much to eat. One night while we were in this barn I got to looking around and found a carrot bed. We had all we could eat that night.

"The next morning I got up and was rolling up my two blankets. As I made each roll, I would put a carrot in the blanket. Some of the other prisoners said they would kill me if I got caught. I said I may as well be killed as starve to death. We started out that morning. The sun was coming up and it was pretty warm. I reached back and got a carrot and one of the other guys said, 'Hey Doug, give us a carrot.' I said, 'If I am going to get shot over them I am going to eat them.'"

Stalag IIIA, February 1945–April 21, 1945

After traveling for about a week the prisoners arrived at Stalag IIIA at Luckenwalde. "It was a big camp and crowded, too. We had to sleep on a concrete floor for about two weeks and then there were a few empty beds. They had made the bunks six high. It was better sleeping except for the body lice. We were infested with them. They fed us soup once a day. Sometimes all it was was hot water. We used it to take a hot bath with instead of drinking it.

"The Russians were treated a lot worse then we were. They carried dead out of their compound everyday. They just starved them. We had grass soup one morning. None of us would eat it. This Russian came over to our barracks with a pot. We would just pour the soup in his pot as we passed. He was happy as could be. The Russians would go out and work. They would steal what they could and bring it back to the camp for trade. We traded, but the most valuable item was cigarettes. You could have bought your way out of camp with enough of the cigarettes."

Each night the artillery fire in the distance signaled to the prisoners

Top: Interior of the tent quarters at Stalag IIIA, Luckenwalde, Germany (National Archives). *Bottom*: Prisoners in the barrack at Stalag IIIA (National Archives).

Top: French hospital patients in a German prison camp taken over by the 3rd U.S. Army Troops in Limburg, Germany (National Archives, Washington, D.C.). *Bottom*: Tent quarters of Stalag IIIA (National Archives).

that the front was getting closer. Then on April 21, 1945, Ed woke up in the early morning. It was quiet. The artillery fire had stopped. He and the other prisoners walked out into the yard and found that the Nazi guards were gone. They were silent as they looked at each other, but they knew that the day they had prayed for had finally came. The end of the war.

The Liberation, April 21, 1945

"The Russians finally came in with tanks and knocked the fence down. They left an old truck and told us if we couldn't go eat now it was our own fault. We went out and found some livestock and started doing our own butchering. The Russians came with their own women. When they weren't shooting, they were getting on the Sherman tanks we had given them. The women were drinking vodka and yelling and laughing.

"We went into the Russian compound and it was amazing. They were starving to death in those compounds, but they had drawn some of the most beautiful pictures on the walls that I have ever seen.

"When those Russians got out and went to town there were some Germans really hurting. They were out for revenge. We were around the camp for a few days and there weren't any Americans coming around so a couple of my buddies and I took off for the front. We finally caught up with some GI trucks and they took us to an airfield. We boarded a C-47 and were flown to Camp Lucky Strike in France. I had lost 38 pounds."

Homeward Bound, June 1945–October 31, 1945

On June 6, 1945, Ed boarded a boat for home. "They assigned several of us to CP [command post] duty just as soon as we took off. We got back in the storage room and I noticed a gallon can of pineapples. I thought, I haven't had them in a long time, and opened them up and started eating. Some of the other guys opened up what they liked and started eating. The officer in charge never said a word, even though we weren't supposed to do it. One day he came in and we told him that we had been assigned to the best duty we ever had. He just laughed.

"When we got back to the States I finally made it to Chicago and got 60 days' leave with orders to report back to Texas. I found out that my folks had thought I was dead. A while after I had been captured, they got a telegram from the war department that I was missing in action. Then a little later they got a letter that I wrote from Stalag IIIA. Well, when the Russians were coming and they took the 30 of us out into that little town, the Russians attacked. I didn't know it, but my cousin was in the camp, was liberated and got home long before I did. My folks let him see the letter and he told them that he had been in the camp. There were a lot of the prisoners that had been killed. They then thought I was one of them. They sure were glad to see me."

POINT OF INTEREST

In late December 1944, sixty American officers in Stalag XIIA were killed during an American B-29 air raid on Limburg. Stalag XIIA was located only 600 yards from a marshaling yard that was the intended target.

CORPORAL RALPH L. LAPE, SR.
U.S. ARMY AIR FORCE

Headquarters, 5th Air Base Group
Captured During the Japanese
Invasion of the Philippines
Prisoner of War
May 10, 1942–September 5, 1945
Mindanao, Kawasaki, and Nigata

A Matter of Age, 1939

Ralph Lape had such an interest in planes that he wanted to enlist in the Army Air Corps. The only thing stopping him was his age. He discussed the problem with his mother and the two paired up and lied about his age so he could enlist. It worked and Ralph went into the Army through Jefferson Barrack on December 2, 1939. He was shipped to the 19th Bomb Group, Hamilton Air Base in San Francisco, California. After eight weeks of basic training he was sent to aviation school to work on aircraft engines. He became an aircraft engine mechanic.

The unit received orders to Tacoma, Washington. Ralph didn't want to go because he liked California. He transferred to the Headquarters Squadron, 5th Air Base Group, at Hamilton Air Base. In a short time, the unit moved to Utah and took over a portion of Salt Lake City's Airport and started a wing there. They trained for months in the Salt Lake Flats. Then the unit moved again, this time to Fort Douglas, Utah, and started a wing at that location and trained for almost a year. Finally, in the fall of 1941 the unit received orders for the Philippines.

The Philippine Islands,
November 1941–December 7, 1941

Security was tight because of concern of the Japanese threat of war and it wasn't until Ralph's unit left the Hawaiian Islands after being transferred from Utah in the middle of November 1941 that they learned their destination. It was "Plum." Plum was a code name for the Philippine Islands. They traveled in blackout until they reached the destination on Thanksgiving Day. "We stayed at Fort McKinley for about two weeks and found out that we were going to take over Clark Air Base. By the time the two weeks were up, that had been changed. We were going to the island of Mindanao and set up there. They moved us by ship to the island and we set up on the Plato of Del Monte.

"Mindanao is the largest of the southern islands of the Philippines. This island is about 500 miles south of Luzon. Most of the air bases were in that area and American commanders realized they needed bases other than those at Luzon, so it was decided to build a base on Mindanao.

"There was a big field and we worked on it to make a runway for B-17s. I was a 747, which meant that I was an aircraft mechanic on the ground and an aerial gunner in the air. About a week after I got there, I saw General [Douglas] MacArthur board a submarine, and as he was going aboard he turned and told us, 'I shall return.' The only problem was he didn't tell us when. We knew something was up because he was leaving. We learned later that he had gone to Australia to set up a base defense."

The Attack, December 8, 1941–May 9, 1942

"We started running missions out over the Pacific and we had completed three missions. We were sent out on our fourth mission to check on some unidentified boats that were approaching the islands. They ended up being the intersteamers (local boats). We were coming in off of our fourth mission in a Douglas bat. It was a twin engine bomber built by Douglas Aircraft; we called it a Bucket of Bolts. We had an aerial engineer aboard, a master sergeant by the name of Pappy Nettles. I was riding as upper tail gunner. We had about a ninety-five percent overcast, and because of a quick break in the clouds, Nettles saw four airplanes flying. They were fighter planes, but that is all we could tell. We landed and taxied up to the end of the runway and the pilot cut the engines. As they died down, I heard engines. I yelled and asked the rest of the crew if they heard the engines. They did and I said, 'Them's not ours.' They weren't. They came down out of the sun right at us. They were the four planes that Nettles had spotted, four Japanese Zeros. They cut loose with the guns. We jumped out of the plane and ran for the trench nearby. They were spaced so that when one would fire and circle the next plane was firing, so we couldn't get out of the trench. On the third pass they hit the plane and set it on fire and it burnt up. The Japs pretty much destroyed the entire Air Force all over the Philippines with the attack, mainly because we didn't have many planes there to start with.

"After the attack we didn't have a plane to fly so they assigned me to twin .50-caliber guns on the airstrip. We had built a hangar back into solid rock where we put our P-40s. The Japanese were trying to lob bombs into the hangar, but they never did get the job done.

"I was there for four days and Pappy Nettles came over and got me. He told me that I had been assigned with him to a P-40. We were moved into the Maramag Forest for protection. The forest was so dense that planes could not be detected from the air. We made several missions and fought day after day. Supplies were low. We were running out of food and ammunition, but we kept resisting until May 1942."

The Surrender, May 10, 1942

"General Wainwright, who had taken over the command of the Philippine Islands, got on the radio. In the northern part of the Philippines the American troops had already surrendered. General Wainwright gave a message ordering us to surrender, because if we didn't, the Japs were going to kill all the other prisoners. On the second day he gave a message again, but this time he also sent an officer escorted by Japanese down to meet with us. Our commander decided we should surrender, and we did on May 10, 1942. They gathered all of us up and we had to go to a village north of Maramag Forest called Malaybalay."

The First Six Months, May 1942–October 1942

"We were there for six months. The village had a barracks that the Filipinos had used and that's where they put us. The barracks was surrounded by barbed wire. We slept on the barracks floor. They fed us rice stew in camp. There were a lot of worms in it and at first we started to try to pick them out, but after a while we just ate worms and all. Once in while we would get a small piece of fish. Rice cakes on occasion.

"They marked us off in sections of ten and told us that if any one man escaped out of the ten the other nine would be shot. They kept their word, too. Several men tried to escape and they would march us out and make us watch them beat men to death or just shoot them. On one occasion, I can remember two men had escaped. They made them dig their own graves. Then they staked them up in front of the grave and shot them and then shot them again in the head after they were already dead. Filipinos covered them with dirt, but the Japs acted like the dead men should have covered themselves, too.

"I saw every horrible inhuman thing that the Japs did, but beheading of a prisoner was the worst. I had two friends that were brothers from West Plains, Missouri, that were in the Bataan Death March. They told me that when they were on the march that the Japs wouldn't let them stop and get a drink of water. They forced them to march for several days and they said that these Jap trucks would come by and Jap soldiers would swing their rifles and hit men in the head as they passed. A lot of men died from head injuries. They bayoneted several of them. One man was in a line and the Japs didn't think the line was straight so they took the man on the end of the line and put him in front of the rest of the soldiers and shot him.

"After we had been in the camp for a while, they began to break us up in groups. At first I didn't know what was going on, but then I figured it out. The Japs were putting those of us that were airmen or men that had technical jobs into one group. They didn't want anybody there that might be able to escape and help out our own side. They were going to ship us to Japan."

Bilibid Prison, October 1, 1942

On October 1, 1942, two hundred and seventy-five prisoners of war, including Ralph, boarded the freighter *Ama Maru* and sailed for Manila. They arrived on October 4, 1942. They were paraded though the streets of Manila to Bilibid Prison. "We were there for a few days. I never knew that I would see a skeleton walk, but they can because I saw it there. No wonder through, because at this prison the diet was strictly rice. Two small bowls given at breakfast, lunch, and dinner. Some of the prisoners were lying on bare floors in the barracks and were covered with flies. Some were dying, some suffered from untreated wounds, and many were ill from the lack of food. Many of the men were slapped around by the Japs. On one occasion we stood in the pouring rain for an hour during roll call as punishment. We never were sure what it was that we did. After about a week's stay at this camp we boarded a boat for Japan."

The Hell Ship Tottori Maru, October 6, 1942–November 12, 1942

On October 6, 1942, Ralph's group of two hundred and seventy-five prisoners along with fifteen hundred POWs from Luzon were crammed aboard the *Tottori Maru*. "The captain of the ship said that we were not prisoners of war, but guests of the emperor. 'We are taking you to Japan where we can feed you better because we took a lot of food off of the island of Corregidor,' the Japanese captain explained. That was a lie because I talked to some guys there and they were down to their last food when they surrendered. We started out of Manila. We were out to sea about three days before we got to Formosa. The conditions were terrible. Below decks it was extremely hot. The men had trouble breathing and several men died from suffocation. The Jap guards passed a bucket around for them to relieve themselves and often it was overflowing before it was emptied. We got small portions of rice while we were on the ship, but it was not near enough to eat.

"On the third day just before arriving at Formosa an American sub attacked us. They fired two torpedoes and the Japs managed to maneuver the ship and the torpedoes missed. We landed at Formosa. They took us off the ship and hosed us down with a fire hose. We stayed there for several days waiting on a convoy. The conditions in Formosa weren't much better than the Philippines, but they sure beat the conditions on the ship. We could get air and we had been washed off, even if it was with ice cold water out of a fire hose.

"Several days later we boarded the ship again and arrived on November 9, 1942, at Chosin, Korea. Most of the POWs from Luzon disembarked here and were taken to a camp at Mukden, Manchuria. Then from there to Japan. We lost a lot of prisoners. We had been stuffed down in the hole with so many they couldn't even lie down. We had to carry a lot of them out and bury them at sea. They had canvas bags we wrapped them in and dumped them overboard.

"I was one of the lucky ones on the trip because I got to stay on top of the deck. They had a hog pen with about three hogs in it and that's where I stayed the whole trip until we got to Japan. Once we got to Japan we were passing a large naval base and when we passed it they made all of us go below deck. It wasn't so bad by then because so many men had died that there was a lot of room below decks. There was a lot of room, but the lower decks were horrible. It stunk from men throwing up. Many of the men had dysentery and there was waste everywhere. They made us stay down there until we passed the naval base and then shortly after that, those of us that had survived the trip arrived at Tokyo Harbor."

Camp Kawasaki, November 12, 1942–July 25, 1945

This camp was located about three miles from Tokyo. The camp held American, British, Italian, and Norwegian prisoners. The living barracks were approximately 18 feet by 75 feet and housed about 120 prisoners. The barracks were built out of wood and covered with shingles or tree bark. Some of the barracks were two-story. Most of the barracks were divided into three sections with each prisoner allowed about 30 by 73 inches for living quarters and stowing clothes.

The floors were wooden in some, but the buildings with dirt floors did not have proper drainage, which caused flooding when it rained. During the winter ice would form under the mats in the sleeping area and would have to be washed down by the prisoners during their days off in order to get rid of fleas and lice. The barracks had a three by three foot fire pit in the center of a section with a small amount of wood allowed during the evening.

The latrines were in a separate wood building large enough to accommodate 30 men at a time. They were called the straddle trenches. The trenches had no drainage so they had to be dipped out. This was distributed to the country side. The open trench caused flies and maggots to accumulate and they crawled around the building and into the living quarters.

The main diet was rice and barley. It was given to the prisoners in small portions. A Japanese Lieutenant, Lieutenant Myazaki, was often in authority in the camp. Some of the other guards at the camp were Mizuno, Shiozawa, Watanabe (nicknamed Porky the Pig), Saito (nicknamed Buck Tooth), Kondo, and Kuriyama.

"We boarded a train to Kawasaki and walked three miles to our new quarters at Camp Kawasaki–Tokyo Area Prisoner of War Camp Number 2. They had barracks there that we stayed in. We had wooden bunks to sleep on. Our food consisted of rice and steamed barley. We were in the camp for about a week when we were assigned work details at the Nippon Steel Mill. The first job I had was working on the railroad. We made railroad tracks. We were on the tracks with civilians. We worked at this job every day. We would get up before daylight, walk to the plant, and work 10 to 12 hours a day, and then return to the barracks. On our first Christmas at the camp the Japs let us take a day off. They allowed us part of a British Red Cross parcel, an apple, a tangerine, and some cigarettes. Although we did get part of a Red Cross parcel on occasion, the food wasn't enough to compensate for the daily hard labor. By the Christmas of 1943, I had lost 50 pounds. We continued the same routine day after day.

"Then on November 1, 1944, a B-29 was seen flying over Tokyo and the first air raid was sounded. From that point on Americans started flying missions day and night over Japan. They used incendiary bombs and burnt houses and buildings all around. The steel mill was shut down for a while, so we were put to work cleaning up the mess after each bombing.

"One day we were cleaning up the area and a couple of our guys wrote V for victory on one of the walls of the hospital. There were a couple of Japanese that could read English and they told the guards. That night when we got back to the camp the Japanese called all of us out and put us in formation. They made us stand there night and day for three days. A lot of the men would fall. The Japs would come over and use rifle butts and beat the prisoners. After three days the men who wrote the V sign finally came forward. They were taken out and executed.

"The next day we went back to work. Ted Venable and I were working on this railroad and they put this older Jap civilian in charge of us to do some different clean up details. He would take us and tell us what to do and we would do it. He was good to us and we liked him. It was in the winter of '45 and the ovens in the plant were warm. We got our bowl of steamed barley and after that we laid down by one of the stoves and went to sleep. The next thing I knew someone was kicking me. I looked up and it was a high ranking Jap officer that was inspecting the plant. He yelled at us and we got up. They slapped us around a little bit. The old Jap guard was hard of hearing and he was asleep. He didn't hear it. They pulled him up and beat him until he couldn't walk.

"That was the way that they punished each other. If one of them messed up they would appoint a person with the next highest rank to beat them. Anyway, they took us back to the barracks and they made us stand out in front of the barracks. They sent this big Jap down and he started in on Ted first. He liked to use his judo and he would hit him. He had a big bamboo stick that he was using, too. I thought that Ted had more sense, but he was kinda asking for it. This Jap would kick him down and Ted would just jump up and get back in formation. The Jap would knock him down. Ted would get back up and stick that chin out for him to hit again. 'Ted when he knocks you down, stay down.' Ted wouldn't do it, but after several knock downs he finally stayed.

"Then he started in on me. He hit me with the stick and used judo. I went with the hits and he never did knock me down. I think it was because he was tired. Finally, he just walked off. Ted looked at me and said, 'I'm better than them damn Japs and I won't bow to them.'

"At the steel mill we had different officers and the higher the rank the more stripes they had on their caps. This Jap picked me to follow this civilian worker around that had an acetylene torch. He showed me how he wanted his torch disassembled and put away. He told me that he wanted me to put it away every time he finished. I did this every day for a long time. Then one day he told me to put the torch up and I started pulling the lines in and wrapping them like he told me. I had my back to him and all at once he started yelling at me and hit me across the back of the neck. It was such a surprise and before I thought I swung and hit him. I stood up and faced him and he started at me. He was a smaller man than I was, and I grabbed him by the arms and put my legs together so he couldn't hit me in the groin.

"There were orders out and placed all over the bulletin boards that if any of us struck a Japanese guard that it was punishable by death. I thought that I had had it. There was another Japanese guard that was in the plant that really liked me. Ray Kellem from West Plains, Missouri, came over with the guard and they started talking with the boss. They were talking in my favor. They told him that I was a good worker and I didn't cause any trouble. They got him to settle down. When the guard came in the civilian didn't tell the guard. For three days after that I was really sweating it out because I thought they would kill me, but they didn't.

"I did see them take a man that had stolen some sugar out of a mess hall and beat him night and day for two or three days. He was an older man like Pappy Nettles and it was really hard on him. His head swelled up and we thought he would die, but he made it.

"We didn't get anything to eat but steamed barley and carrot soup. We never got salt so every once in a while we would sneak down and get a bucket of water from the ocean. When the water settled, we would get the salt from the side of the bucket. It was the only way we had of getting any salt.

"The bombing was bad and the Japs started making weapons out of steel for the civilians. They told us that we would all be killed if the Americans invaded Japan. They just simply thought we had to die.

"We watched as the planes came over and bombed Tokyo. The Jap guards beat us for it. They were always beating us for something, but they were worse when the bombing started. Then in the middle of April 1945, B-29s flew over our camp area at approximately 6,000 feet and hit Tokyo. It was a large air raid and it knocked out our water and electricity.

"For this raid we weren't beaten. The Japs had a better payback. They gave us the news that President Roosevelt had died. We were saddened by the news, but at the same time we had to laugh to ourselves because the Japs tried to convince us that they were now going to win the war.

"About a month later, in May, we had the largest raid to date. Approximately 600 planes dropped incendiary bombs on Tokyo. The Japs wouldn't let us go to the bomb shelters. Luckily no one in the camp was injured.

"In July, the camp was hit by heavy bombing which lasted all night. Twenty-two prisoners were killed and our camp was completely destroyed. The entire area was a total mess. We were moved to another camp."

Camp Nigata, July 1945–September 1945

"We were moved to Camp Nigata, about 500 miles northwest of Tokyo. All we did was unload boats. We had to walk for a mile and a half to work. We unloaded boats all day. The boats were full of food. We worked day after day unloading the food, but we never got any of it. I never received a beating at this camp. All in all, it was a better camp than the first one.

"It was getting close to the end of the war and the Japs started thinning out. They began to lay off of us. When you bragged on one of these guards, they would answer a lot of questions before they thought. They told us about Germany surrendering."

Surrender, August 16, 1945

"When the A-bombs were dropped, we didn't know it, but we did know that something had happened. They were always bragging about shooting down planes or something, but one day it was different. The Japs wouldn't even look at us. They looked down and were really humble. Then we found out that they had surrendered."

Liberation

Ralph and his fellow prisoners were not liberated from the camp; they just walked out after two American officers arranged their release. The Americans marched out of the camp to a train station and demanded to be taken to Tokyo. While disembarking the train, Ralph and some of the other Americans noticed two armed soldiers and a Red Cross girl. Some of the guys ran over and hugged and kissed on the girl. She laughed. Ralph was taken to Yokohama where he was fed, deloused and given medical treatment and new clothes.

Home, September 1945–July 1946

Ralph boarded a C-47 and flew to Okinawa, where some of the Japanese were still dug in, then to Manila, because MacArthur wanted all able-bodied men to come back so he could show them that we had taken it back. They finally returned to San Francisco. A train took Ralph to a hospital in Iowa, where he stayed until he recuperated.

He returned to his home in Chaffee, Missouri, and he was discharged in February 1946.

POINTS OF INTEREST

War Crimes Trial

During the war crimes trials a number of those in authority at Camp Kawasaki were tried and convicted. Lt. Myazaki received forty years in prison, Mizuno received five years and Shiozawa received twenty years. Watanabe "Porky the Pig" received forty years, Saito "Buck Tooth" received thirty years. Kondo received one year, and Kuriyama received life in prison. All were to serve their terms at Sugamo prison. By 1958, all the Japanese guards were released from prison.

Hell Ships

The following are examples of the more than 130 Japanese vessels used to transport Allied POWs.

Tattori Maru: 11 dead. Departed Manila on October 8, 1942, with 1,202 American POWs. Stopped at Formosa, Japan, and arrived at Manchuria on November 11, 1942.

Umeda Maru: 15 dead. Departed Manila on November 7, 1942, with 1,500 American POWs. Arrived in Japan, November 1942.

Nagato Maru: 157 dead. Departed Manila on November 7, 1942, with 1,700 POWs. Arrived in Japan on November 25, 1942. Seven died en route; 150 dying men left on dock were never seen again.

Taga Maru: 70 dead. Departed Manila on September 1943 with 850 American POWs. Unknown arrival date.

Shinyo Maru: 668 dead. Departed Zamboanga, Mindanao, on December 3, 1944, with 750 American POWs. Torpedoed by USS *Paddle* on September 7, 1944. Only 83 POWs survived.

Haru Maru: 39 dead. Departed Manila on October 3, 1944, with 1,100 American POWs. Arrived in Takao, Formosa, on October 25, 1944.

Arisan Maru: 1,795 dead. Departed Manila on October 10, 1944, with 1,800 American POWs. Torpedoed by USS *Snook* on October 24, 1944.

Oryoku Maru: 1,426 dead. Departed Manila on December 13, 1944, with 1,800 American POWs. Sunk by U.S. carrier planes off Bataan Peninsula on December 15, 1944.

— 11 —

LIEUTENANT THOMAS J. HART
U.S. ARMY

Port Battalion G, 5307th, 475th, and
124 Cavalry, L Troop
Captured During an Offensive in Burma
After Being Left for Dead
Camp Hosi
January–March 1945
Escaped

Fighting for One's Country, March 1943

At the age of 17, Tom Hart went to the Army headquarters to enlist. One of the Army officers wanted to know why Tom wanted to join at such a young age. Tom replied, "Because I want to fight for my country." The Army enlisted Tom, but he wasn't allowed to leave for active duty until he turned 18.

On his 18th birthday, March 1943, Tom received orders to report to Fort Benjamin Harrison in Indianapolis, Indiana, for a physical. He passed the physical and was sent to Fort Lawson in Seattle, Washington. They had to clear a wooded area for the tents and never did transfer from the tents to the new barracks being built. They completed their training in basic warfare in about eight weeks.

Tom was then assigned to 286th Port Company A as a longshoreman. He was trained in ship repair and loading and unloading ships. He recalled, "I thought I was going to carry a rifle all the time, but the only time I ever shot a rifle was on the range during basic.

"After we completed the training we were supposed to get a 15-day

155

furlough, but instead they shipped our unit to Skagway, Alaska. We loaded pipe for a pipeline and stayed in Alaska for about three months."

In June 1943, Tom's unit returned to Seattle and the men were given 15 day furloughs. After the furlough, he returned and had orders to report to San Francisco, where his unit was to catch a ship to the South Pacific. They were in San Francisco for a couple of weeks and then boarded the USS *Hermitage* and headed west in October 1943. During the journey across the Pacific, Tom would acquire the nickname Sugar Foot. Tom, an ordained minister, used the word in place of swear words. A few weeks later, Sugar Foot and his unit arrived in Freemantle, Australia. Tom saw his first kangaroo, enjoyed the white beaches and was entertained by a show of musicians and dancers in the next four days, and then it was time to pull out once again.

A Journey to India

Tom's ship was on the high seas for four days when it developed mechanical trouble. The drive shaft broke and the men coasted into the island of Bora Bora. It took five days to repair the ship. The ship headed for India, zigzagging all the way across the Indian Ocean. Tom turned nineteen during this 40 day trip to Bombay in November 1943.

Tom and his unit loaded aboard trains and headed for Calcutta, India, where the battalion was to work on the docks. When they arrived at the docks, Tom was shocked. "I saw all these men and women walking around with mouths as red as blood. I thought there was something wrong with them. This has to be the worst place in the world to be. Later, I found out I was wrong. They chewed a tobacco that had red juice instead of brown. I felt better after that. On the docks we unloaded rifles, bombs, tanks, and ammunition. I never expected to see any of it again when it left the dock, but I did. The war kept getting worse and worse. By the type and amount of supplies coming in I knew we were going to make an invasion against the Japs in jungle terrain somewhere."

Sabotage

There were Japanese sympathizers on the dock. They would constantly feed information to the Japanese army about the amount and types of supplies Tom's unit was moving on the dock. They also sabotaged the area. Tom recalled, "I had coolies working for me and I treated them good. They would really work well for me. One day I noticed this Hindu sitting on a pallet. I went up to him and asked him what right he had to just sit around while the rest of us worked. He said, 'Go to hell,' in English, and when he did he realized he messed up and took off running. I chased him all over the docks and through warehouses and finally with the help of the MPs we caught him. He was a spy for the Japs.

"That same night while I working on the docks, I noticed this crane with a pallet of steel hanging over the dock. The coolies were working under the pallet and I kept watching this pallet. Sparks started flying and the strands on the cable began to break. Just as the last one snapped I ran over and knocked the coolies out of the way. Had I not, they would have been killed.

"The next day they took me off the docks and told me that I couldn't go back on the docks anymore. I asked the lieutenant why he was doing it to me. He said, 'Sugar Foot, there are spies on the dock that are out to kill you. I can't let you go back any more.' I was devastated."

Merrill's Marauders

Tom was depressed from being relieved of his duties on the docks and his resistance broke down, which then developed into a severe fever. After three weeks in the hospital he was assigned to a construction job building barracks. He hated it. Then one day a famous unit was asking for volunteers. "I was walking past one of the barracks and I saw a notice on the side of the barracks. It stated that if there was anyone interested in volunteering for the 5307th Infantry, Merrill's Marauders, sign here. Well I put my name down there in a hurry. I was third on the list.

"A few days later all the volunteers met in a theater on the base with one of the officers. He told us that if we were volunteers for the Marauders that we would be on combat duty. That it was going to be rough. He gave us one last chance to leave if we weren't interested. A large group got up and left. When the theater cleared there were about 50 of us left. We were told we would have our orders in two days and that we weren't going to receive any training because they needed us right now."

The First Combat

"Boy, two days later we had our combat gear and were headed for the train. My old lieutenant came up as I was leaving and told me that he would give me a sergeant's rating if I would change my mind. I told him that I never changed my mind. He offered me staff sergeant and that sounded good, but I turned him down. We boarded the train and started across India. Somewhere in India we boarded trucks and finally arrived at our destination. The minute we got to the destination we were being fired at by the Japs. I had an M-1 and cartridge belt and I jumped from the truck. I loaded a clip and learned how to fire that rifle immediately. It seemed like I was shooting in the air because I had never shot a weapon and I had a talk with myself about settling down and not wasting bullets. We were pinned down by the Japs overnight, but the next morning they were gone.

"We started assaulting the airport the next morning. The Japs were well fortified and fought for every inch of ground until we finally took the airfield. They had torn up the air fields, but we were told the combat engineers would come in and fix it.

"After we took the air field we were regrouped and started sending the original Marauders home. There was only about three hundred of us left. We defended the airfield and were hit by several suicide planes and constantly had to guard against Jap snipers."

The Mars Task Force, July 1944–January 1945

"The 475th Infantry began to train even harder to be offensive combat men. Some of us began to move out. Those of us that had been trained by the Marauders had a replacement unit to come in, known as the 124th Cavalry, from Texas. These men were extremely good with horses, but they never had any other training. Those of us who had mules were the ones we had loaded in Calcutta, when I was in the 508th Port Battalion. The 124th Cavalry knew how to fight like cavalry, but they knew nothing about the jungles. Those of us who had some earlier, bitter experiences in jungle fighting were dispersed among the cavalrymen and the 475th Infantry.

"Maybe these men knew nothing about the jungle, but they were very quick to catch on. The Mars Task Force became even meaner than the Marauders. Those Texans weren't afraid of anything. They were used to snakes and other prairie animals because they were a border patrol outfit from the 56th Cavalry Brigade in Texas, which exists to this day.

"The Mars Task Force was made a new unit in July 1944. The name was acquired after a diary from a mortally wounded Japanese soldier. His diary read, 'Their men are all from Mars. They're everywhere. We don't know where they will strike next.' Now it was time for more jungle combat training. The Japanese were gaining more and more ground. General Cheves was our command leader at the time, then came Colonel Hazeltine and Colonel Jefferies. These three courageous men were the ones who thought we were ready to go into combat. They had a lot of faith in the men of the Mars Task Force. They were absolutely right. By now, I was becoming a seasoned combat fighter in the jungles along with the other brave and fearless men in our unit. I believe that we were more deadly than any of the fighting men known at the time.

"I was assigned to Troop L of the 124th Cavalry, under the leadership of Captain Thompson. Our troop was known as the front scouts, while the G, F and I troops of the 124th Cavalry were the flanks. We all had our particular jobs to do in our newly organized unit. Major Blair, Captain Thompson, and Lieutenant Rhoads were our troop leaders. I was placed in the squad with Sgt. Eggers and Corporal Fields.

"I became known as 'Padre' because of my past experience of being a minister of the Nazarene faith, and I had taken our chaplain's place on many occasions because he was busy elsewhere, in the fighting, where he was needed most. Chaplain Gump was a very busy man, behind the lines, serving the wounded and other personnel.

"The Mars Task Force began to lay down a hard fight against the Japs. In August 1944, a rather light skirmish took place. The Japs were driven back by a surprise attack from F and L troops. It didn't last long, because we were surrounding the Jap forces in small groups to cut off the supply routes, then taking a little time to mop up the pockets that had been cut off from their main forces. It was very effective, because the enemy would run rather than fight, and we ran, too, to regroup. The Japs thought that the Americans had regained their combat readiness when they were able to infiltrate where ever they wanted to. In December 1944, I was given a field commission as chaplain with the rank of first lieutenant. Colonel Hazeltine promoted based on performance in the field.

"It was with pride that we began the warfare of seek and destroy and run. This was done well most of the time. We were trained for this kind of battle fighting. The jungles became our friend, as well as our enemy. The enemy side had the same problems as the Marauders. Pestilence and hunger were taking their toll on the Japs as much as it was on the Americans. It was pestilence that was hurting us more than the actual combat fighting, now. The monsoons were hitting us hard. It would rain for days and days, then the sweltering heat would hit us. It was as if the lurking jungle was lashing out at us.

"On one occasion we camped near a stream. The cobras were thick in the area. We didn't know this until the next day. Dick Thompson and I, who were the BAR [Browning automatic rifle] men, woke up and while we were shaking the water from our blankets, Dick noticed a cobra was erect and ready to snap at him. We finally got enough courage to get close enough to cut its head off with our machetes. Some of the men weren't so lucky.

"We had to stay in this area another night, because we got the word that the Japs were heading our way, and we were to destroy them. The next day we received orders to move out, because the Japs moved in another direction. We were relieved to hear this, for we were anxious to get out of cobra country.

"The jungle was an enemy, but also a friend. We were headed south toward Bhamo when we were alerted that a company of Japs was secured around the town of Bhamo. We began our cautious way in the jungle. We found several encampments of Japs and ran each of them out. The jungle hid us from the enemy, and in our training we were to sneak up on the enemy at night, and hit them when they least expected it.

"Our squad was to secure a Buddhist Temple that the Japs had made into a fortress. We called for the artillery. Then we made a rush toward the temple. In the holes that the artillery made in the walls we were able to throw hand grenades into the temple. We ran into the temple when the shooting stopped, but the Japs had left under fire. We secured the temple and made it safe without one bullet being fired after we got inside. The jungles helped us achieve our goals most of the time.

"Just after securing Bhamo, we took a rest period. Dick and I decided we would go into town and look around. As we were sightseeing, we got word that we were to pull out the next morning. All men were to report back to their squads at once.

"Well, we knew that something was about to happen. The next morning we pulled out, and we walked for two days — about twenty to forty miles — with hardly any rest. We catnapped at night, and we would get moving before daylight. We were careful not to leave anything uncovered, such as ration containers, chewing gum wrappers, or cigarettes, because we knew that we were surrounded by Japs.

"We went down the mountain and got caught in the valley with nowhere to go. Someone had made a mistake on the map. The Japs were looking down our throats. We knew we had to get back on high ground. Desperately, we began to move out with our mules, for they were carrying the ammunition and other materials that we couldn't carry up the mountain stream. Our mules would sometimes slip off the ridges and fall into the water. We had to have them.

"Finally, after eight to ten hours of hard walking, we made it to the top. We thought we were safe. We made camp. The order came that no one was to eat or drink anything. No noise was to be made at all. For once, the sound of night birds and animals were a blessing, so no one could hear our mules snore. It was all blended in together.

"We were prepared for the worst and another officer was evacuated because of wounds. In one second his groin was shot off completely. Sgt. Knight was seriously wounded, and then the fighting stopped. F troop was completely wiped out, except for about 30 men. They really took a bad beating. The Japs had fallen back into the lower country, but they were

161

still on one hill. Troop L was to secure that hill. The Japs had just beaten F Troop and these Japs were the same bunch that had done it.

"We all lined up at the foot of the hill. Every man was to be on his own from now on. Then came the word, 'move out.' It seemed that the whole world was shooting guns. The heavy machine guns were shooting over our heads. The artillery quit coming in. All you could hear was screaming in warlike fashion. We were all fighting with bars and .30-caliber machine guns. "All of a sudden the artillery fell on us. The line had to stop, for we had gotten into the sights of the Nambu [Japanese machine guns] the Japs were firing on us. One by one, men began to fall. I noticed Wayne Christmas stop. He was by me. He pointed in front of me on the ground. A Nambu was aimed in our direction and the dirt was spitting up toward us. I stopped and zeroed in on the direction the bullets were coming, and finally the Nambu stopped.

"In the meantime, Tom called out to me to run, because I would get the next artillery shell. He no sooner got it out when I felt something hit me from behind."

Being Wounded

"As I was lying on the ground being left behind from the main body of my comrades, I was being picked up by four or five men. They dragged me over to my buddy Wackler, who lay dead with his shirt pulled open and at least three bullet holes in his chest. I knew that he was dead.

"While I was being carried down the hill, I heard these men talking. They were not using English language. These were Japanese soldiers. I knew then that I had been taken prisoner. Fear gripped me like nothing before in this world. I wasn't afraid of the men, as much as I was afraid of what they could or would do to me. Many times we had gone through a village where we would see the body of an American soldier hanging from a tree limb. His penis had been cut off and stuffed in his mouth as he was dying.

"I could mention other atrocities that the Japs did to the villagers who were sympathetic toward the American fighting men. Inhuman treatment was forced upon our missionaries, also. Especially bad things were done to the women and girls. The native women were badly treated by the Japanese soldiers. The Japs wanted to win the war, but they never seemed to care how they did it, or how others would feel about the Japanese soldiers and people. They wanted to be superior in every way, above other people. They had no friends among the villagers."

Tom's Story, January 1945–March 1945

"I was thrown to the ground and kicked and beaten with rifles. My head was hurting so badly. I kept feeling a strange sensation in my chest. It felt like fire coming into me. Finally, they quit beating me. I was told to stand up at attention. I tried to stand, but every time I would fall again. Then, someone would hit me again. I tried it five times and then I prayed to God for extra strength to be able to stand up. I got up the strength that I needed, and stood at attention the best way I could.

"One officer noticed that my chest had been bleeding. Even I didn't notice this. He tore my shirt open. I had a piece of shrapnel penetrating my chest bone. He hit that piece of metal with his hand, to see if he could shove it further into my body. I stood there in fright, knowing that he wanted me to fight back, or faint, or to die. Instead of crying out, I prayed for God to let me not feel the pain. I was talking to Jesus Christ the whole time. Somehow, I felt no pain at all, as the officer tried to push the shrapnel through to my inner chest wall. The piece of metal would not move.

"He asked me my name. I gave him my name and serial number, but not my rank, because I had just been awarded my cross as a chaplain, and was made first lieutenant. I thought I had lost my cross. I never felt in my pocket for it. He took my dog tag that had been pinned to my shirt.

"I thought that it was funny that I did not have it around my neck. I never gave it another thought because I didn't really know what had happened to me. All I could remember was that I was tumbling in the air before I lost consciousness on the battlefield.

"As I stood in front of these men, I felt that I was losing consciousness again. I felt hungry, and I was hurting in my head and my chest. I must have passed out then. When I awoke, I found myself in a dark boarded room. I could barely look through the cracks of the wall. I knew

163

that I was a prisoner at that time. I heard men talking. As they got closer and closer, I knew I was in for a beating. I had heard the Japs did this sort of thing to all their prisoners.

"I began to pray for courage and strength. At that moment I felt a sense of strength and power move over me. I was certain that it was the peace of God, with the power of His spirit, coming to me in a place where there was no peace. By the time the soldiers came in the door, I was standing at attention and was saluting them all as they walked in. They knew then that I was able to be interrogated.

"I lost all track of time and days. Nothing seemed important, only to be prepared to live and not to die. I kept this on my mind all the time.

"Then the officer in charge came in to see me. He could speak good English. He said he was my friend, and that he went to college somewhere in California. I didn't know much about California, but I made a small smile. He took it wrong. He hit me in the face. The officer asked me my name, rank, and serial number and what outfit I was with. I gave him my serial number and name only. I told him no more.

"I was told they were taking me from the dark place. They took me in front of the Jap soldiers, so everyone could see an American in captivity. Then I was put in a place that had some more light. This was when the interrogation really started. I was to sit at a table with my hands downward on the table.

"They asked me questions about my outfit. When I refused to tell, they would hit my hands with the butt of a rifle. I would see blood begin to spurt from my fingers and knuckles. No one will ever know how much it hurt. I would not give in and tell them anything. Then, they would pierce my fingers with sharp bamboo sticks. I was hurting really bad and it finally got so bad I would pass out. Then they left me alone for days.

"The officer came in one day and said to me, 'I see you didn't die, you must be a miracle man.' I said nothing at all. He went out. I knew that he was going to try, again, to kill me. I knew I had to escape to stay alive. I had watched my captors very closely, and observed that around late afternoon everyone would be silent. That time of day, hardly anyone was around. It must have been a rest period for the Japanese."

The Escape

"I called for the officer to come and see me. The guard got an officer who could understand English, but he could not speak it. I asked him to come closer to me, that I could tell him all that he wanted to know. He smiled and came closer to me.

"For the first time, I knew that I was going to kill, because that is what we were trained to do. I grabbed him then with my badly bruised arms and hands, I destroyed him. I hid him in the dark park of the Basha. I began to laugh and cry at the same time, hysterically. I couldn't keep quiet. I yelled and screamed and cried and laughed until I got hold of myself and began to pray for forgiveness.

"I felt easier then, and began to relax. I knew I had to get away quickly, now. I kicked a loose board that I had located earlier, and crawled out of the hole to get outside. Just then, a guard saw me. I had to kill him, too. I got on my hands and knees and crawled along a line of escape that I had planned while in the Basha.

"When I got to the jungle, I felt safe. But I knew that there had to be booby traps, so I watched for them closely. When I found the traps, I stepped carefully over them, and I was free. I was soon more deeply into the jungle, and felt free in every way. Now I had time to heal myself. I had a chance to forget my experiences as quickly as possible. I had only the jungle to worry about now. It was better than being afraid I was going to die in a prison camp."

Surviving the Jungle

"After my escape from the Japanese, I began to roam in the jungle in the day, and find open country to sleep at night. I wandered and wandered until I began to get my bearings. I had to decide where and what I must do in order to survive, because I was getting extremely thirsty and hungry. I thought I would die of starvation or thirst. I had no sense of time and days. If I would happen to wander near a village I would run away, because I was afraid of being captured again.

"I thought only of survival. I needed a place to live that would be as safe as possible from the elements of nature. So I decided to build a tree house. While I was wandering around, I found a machete and trench knife that I could use for tools, as well as for weapons.

"I looked for a good tree that had the right kind of limbs for the tree house. When I found the perfect tree, I began to cut bamboo trees and split the bamboo in order to make the floor. In doing so, I found that the bamboo had pure water stored in the fourth section from the ground. It was cool water and tasted good. So I drank water until I nearly burst.

"I got awfully sick after that, but I think I drank too much to start with. I would tie the end of the vine around one piece of bamboo and then make a cross bar. Then I would tie a piece at a time, until I made my floor complete.

"I then wondered how I was going to get it up the tree. This stumped me. I thought that I should have built it in the tree in the beginning. I didn't want to take it apart, so I figured a way to get it up the tree.

"I cut a large vine, and climbed the tree. I looped the vine over the limbs on which I wanted my house to be. Then, I tied one end of the vine to the floor, and pulled on the other end until I got it higher than where I wanted to lace it. I fastened a loose end to a small tree. Then climbed to where I was going to set the floor. I managed to swing it over the limbs, and let it fall into place.

"I left my machete on the ground; I had to shinny down the tree, then climb back up the tree, and start all over again. I swung the floor back and forth until I had the thing in place. At that time, I swung my machete and cut the vine. I just sat there, admiring my new home.

"I didn't know where I was, or why I was there, only that I had left prison camp. I began to drink my water more slowly at this time and rest up after a hard day's work. I sat and said to myself, I will finish tomorrow. As I sat there, it began to get dark. The night birds and animals began to make noise. The monkeys were jumping from one limb to another. I hadn't noticed that I was being watched by the monkeys or birds. There they were, looking at this new neighbor who had just moved in.

"The moon got bright. It was shining through the leaves above me. The night sounds of the jungle made me very sleepy. I forgot about the Japs and prayed my prayers. The Japs had taken my Bible that I carried in my shirt pocket. My mother had given it to me when I left for the service. I could still pray and quote from memory. I felt safe, and fell sound asleep.

"I was awakened when something touched me the next morning. I jumped up and scared the biggest monkey I ever saw up close. When it screamed, it scared me. I thought I would die from the fright. Soon, composure came back and I realized I was in good hands after all. I sat there wishing that the monkey would come back. He did. We were both more careful the next time not to scare each other.

"As the morning went along, I was getting hungrier by the minute so I thought I would climb down from my house to find some food. I'd remembered in jungle training, that there was food to eat, such as roots, berries, and wild lemon. I heard a familiar noise like a jackal growl. I climbed back up the tree and looked down and sure enough there were two jackals looking up at me. They thought they had their breakfast, but I didn't think so.

"I waited and waited until everything got quiet again. I climbed down and started looking for berries or nuts or anything that was edible, but it was to no avail. I found nothing to eat. I was beginning to get too weak to do anything. The next morning, I followed the monkeys to see where they were getting their food. I went into the brush where they were going and sure enough I found some berries. I ate berries for what seemed to be an hour. My hunger went away.

"One day, the monkeys and birds were really restless. Someone was coming. I jumped down from the tree and ran for the jungle. I was glad I did; it was several Jap soldiers. I hid in the brush until they were gone."

Friendly Hands

"Each day, I would cut through the jungle to see where I was. It seemed like an eternity had passed. I heard motors running in the distance and I thought someone was after me. After a while, I would venture closer and closer to the sounds I was hearing. I came to a road and saw a truck going down the road. I saw a star on the side and I knew that it was American.

"I ran to the road. I was waving my hands and screaming at the top of my voice for them to stop. It was a convoy and none would stop until the last truck. The driver got out and asked who I was. I told him my name, rank, and serial number and that I was a chaplain and had escaped from the Japanese. He wouldn't believe me.

"He told me to get in the back of the truck. When I did, I fell on the bed of the truck exhausted. It was getting along in the evening and I asked the men in the back where we were headed. They wouldn't answer me at first. They questioned me about my looks, where I had been, and how I got all the dirt and blood on me.

"I didn't know I was in that condition. They said my hair was all matted with blood and dirt. I didn't believe them. Finally, we got near an airport. They took me into a building where there were nurses and doctors and other medics. It was near dark. I was taken to a room that had cement tubs or something like that. One man had me undress and get into the water. It felt so good to me. It was the first bath I had had in months. He asked me how I got so beat up, but all I said was it was rough.

"He tried to shave me, but my beard was too thick. He tried to use the hair clippers. They pulled too badly, so he got some nurse's scissors, and cut my beard and hair with those. Finally, he was able to shave me. He cut my hair with clippers. My face and head were so swollen that he was afraid to cut my hair very close. Then, the doctor gave me a good physical.

"I stayed in the hospital until they released me to go to Kumming, China. My body was full of lice and other scaly things. My feet were rotten with jungle rot. I wasn't sure how long I had been in the jungle. I know for at least 92 days, for each day I would make a mark on the tree. I don't know the number of days that I was unconscious but those days were obviously not counted. Nevertheless, I lived through it all: dysentery, malnutrition, dehydration, and all."

Kunming, China

After a couple of weeks, Tom boarded a C-47 for India. He stopped at Kunming, China, for a period of time and enjoyed the culture and traditions of the people and land. The visit was not without problems, however, because it was during the time that the communist government was taking over China. The Inland Mission station had to put up a wall around their compound to protect the American missionaries. Tom did what he could to help until he finally was assigned to a general hospital in India.

Home

Tom made it home and was discharged November 5, 1945. Four days later he married Betty Craig. The couple had three sons, Joseph, Jerry, and Jim. All three served in the armed services and two of his sons served in the Vietnam War.

STAFF SERGEANT R. L. HULSEY
U.S. ARMY AIR FORCE

8th Air Force, 93rd Bomb Group, 409th Squadron
Captured After Being Shot Down
Over Solingen, Germany
Prisoner of War
December 1, 1943–May 4, 1945
Stalag 17B

A Volunteer Sets Army Record, August 1940–July 1942

On August 6, 1940, at the age of 18, Russell Hulsey joined the Army. He was a volunteer, patriotic, and by all means ambitious. He completed his basic training, gunner school in Nevada and Armor School in Denver, Colorado. During that time his motivation and leadership qualities repeatedly placed his performance far above his fellow soldiers. One promotion after another finally led him to the rank of staff sergeant. It also led him to a unique title. At the age of 19 he became the youngest staff sergeant in the U.S. Army.

Russell was in a training command until late 1942. By now the war was in full swing and the young staff sergeant wanted to do his part. He volunteered for combat duty and was sent to Tucson, Arizona, and then to Biggs Field at El Toro, California. Upon completion of his training he was sent overseas to a B-24 bomber group.

Combat Duty, July 1942–December 1943

In July 1942, Russell was shipped to Europe as a replacement for the 8th Air Force, 93rd Bomb Group, of the 409th Squadron based in Hardwick, England. Then for a while his unit was based in Bengazi, Libya, and went on several missions in North Africa and other areas in support of the 9th Air Force.

In 1943 a new policy was implemented for the air crews. Completion of 25 bombing missions was the ticket back to the United States. Very few men or crews completed that many missions because of the intense Nazi anti-air defense. For example, in October 1943, the 8th Air Force lost so many planes that the bombing raids were suspended during that month. In November they resumed the raids. Russell, like most of the airmen, wanted to complete his 25 missions and go home, but this time his decision to volunteer worked against him. Russell recalled, "I was assigned to the *Tupelo Lass* and got sick during one of the bombing raids. I wanted to make the mission up in order to get my 25 missions, so I volunteered to go on a bombing run with another crew.

"On December 1, 1943, we took off with a bombing mission to hit a steel mill over Solingen, Germany. At 1:00 P.M. we were flying at 18,000 feet when we were hit with flak. We had to leave the formation with one engine on fire. We dropped below cloud level and were attacked by German fighter planes. One of the gunners was killed during the attack and the plane was severely damaged. The pilot could not control the plane and I was forced to bail out. It was the first time that I had ever bailed out of a plane. I had never gone through E training back in the States.

"As I jumped, I looked up and the plane blew up above me as I fell through the clouds. It was snowing and very cold. As I hit the ground, I could hear a dog barking. The visibility was poor and I had no idea where I was. I gathered up my parachute and hid it in a hay stack. I found a couple of trees that had moss growing on them. I learned that moss grew on the north side of the tree, so I could determine my direction from that. I found a road and begin walking west. Late in the evening after hours of walking I came to some crossroads and noticed a country church. I wanted to get in out of the cold for the night so I decided that this would be a good place to stay. I went inside the church and laid down on the floor at the front pew. About thirty minutes later I heard the door open and someone walk into the church. My heart almost stopped, I was so scared, but I found out that it was an elderly lady that had seen me go into the church. She couldn't speak English so she motioned for me to follow her. She took me to her house and put me in her basement. It was just getting dark outside."

The Capture, December 1, 1943

In a short time the basement door busted open, only this time Russell wasn't so lucky. "I was in the basement for about one hour when German soldiers busted open the door. Someone had spotted her helping me and reported it to the Germans. They shot her and took me to a small building in the village where they kept me overnight. The next morning they took me to a grade school and paraded me in front of the school children. They told them that I was one of the American gangsters that was destroying their country.

"Later that day they put me on a train and sent me to Frankfurt, Germany. I was interrogated there. They asked me about my training, how many planes were in our group, and where we were stationed. All I would give them is my name, rank, and serial number. I had put a picture of my girlfriend in my billfold to carry with me. One of the guards going through it, found the picture and asked me who it was. I told him that it was my girlfriend and that if I made it back to the States I was going to marry her. He said, 'If I had someone that pretty waiting on me I would want to keep my picture.' He stamped the back of the picture and gave it to me. I still have it today."

Forty and Eights

Forty men and eight horses would be a load for the Germans, but not American POWs. They were crammed on the boxcars to the point that they couldn't sit or lie down. They rode for days without food, little water, and with no provisions for relieving themselves. "After the interrogation they placed me and other prisoners on a train and transported us to a prison camp. We were on the train for several days before arriving at the camp. Altogether it had been approximately two weeks since my capture and during that time all I had to eat was dark bread and water. For the next several days it wouldn't get any better. The train was packed with no room to lie down. One corner was used to relieve ourselves and we got no food. After several days we arrived at Stalag 17B near Krems, Austria."

Stalag 17B, December 1943–April 16, 1945

Stalag 17B was located 85 kilometers from Vienna, Austria. The first American prisoners arrived at the camp on October 13, 1943. From that time until April 1945 there was a steady input of prisoners, totaling about 4,300. The camp consisted of 12 compounds, five of them for Americans, the others for Italians, Russians, French, and Serbs. Each compound had four double barracks, 40 feet wide and about 130 feet long, constructed

Stalag 17B in 1944. Photograph taken by a prisoner who had obtained a camera and smuggled it into camp (SSgt. R. L. Hulsey).

on piling 25 to 36 inches off the ground. Each barracks was divided by a washroom which was divided into three partitions. Each washroom had 24 water faucets but usually only three of each six worked. When the faucets broke the Germans refused to replace them, using the excuse that the Americans broke them to hinder the German effort. There was never any hot water to wash clothes or to clean the barracks. Water was turned on one hour in the morning, at noon, and in the evening. The water situation was very poor and there was never enough water for the three hundred men in the barracks.

By the end of the war conditions even became worse. The barracks were built to house approximately 240 and by the end of the war there were at least 400 men crowded into each barracks. There were two barbed wire fences surrounding the camp and watch towers equipped with machine guns at strategic points.

About a month and a half before Russell was captured and sent to Stalag 17B, the first Americans were sent to the camp. The POWs found filthy barracks loaded with bedbugs, fleas, and other varmints. The Nazis had made no attempt to clean or delouse the living quarters before the prisoners arrived. The bunks had large masses of lice eggs and bedbugs, and the prisoners never got rid of the lice and other varmints during the time the camp was open. The Nazis claimed they could get rid of the lice by shaving the prisoners' heads so the lice could not breed in their hair. They shaved their heads during the middle of winter with below zero temperatures. The majority of the men had no caps to cover their heads. They added delousing showers by the time Russell arrived. "The first thing that they did was to run us through a delousing area. They made us take all of our clothes off as they ran us through the showers. Then they shaved our heads and took us to camp.

"There was a total of about 4,000 American prisoners in the camp. They kept us locked in the buildings most of the time and on a few occasions turned their police dogs loose on us in the barracks because they were concerned that we would attempt to escape."

Russell, as many of the prisoners did, became victim to the sub-zero temperatures with frost bite to both hands. The barracks weren't heated and there wasn't anything to burn for heat in the sub-zero weather. The Nazis issued two thin cotton blankets to each man. There was a stove in each barracks but no coal was ever furnished. The only heat generated was by the 300 prisoners in the barracks. Often prisoners slept two and three together in a bunk to stay warm.

During the 18 months that the prisoners were in the camp, they received five showers. When the showers were given four or five men at a time had two to three minutes under the water tap. By the time half of the men had showers the hot water was gone and the remainder had to take showers in ice-cold water.

There were never enough eating utensils. The men were issued a bowl and spoon. If the bowls were broken, they were never replaced. The utensils weren't that much of a problem because there wasn't that much to eat. "We didn't work, but we didn't get much to eat. As many as 17 men had to share a loaf of bread. Of course, the Germans didn't have anything to eat either, so it was difficult to provide for us. They made rutabaga soup, dehydrated cabbage, and sometimes we got half rotten potatoes. The soup and cabbage often had bugs and worms in it. We did get a few Red Cross parcels and some clothing, but for the most part food was very scarce. They would line us up and when we got the Red Cross parcels they would take a bayonet and punch holes in the cans so that you had to eat everything right then. They did that so we couldn't save the food for an escape."

The prisoners spent much of each day waiting on time. One of the things that gave them hope and raised morale for the prisoners during these times was mail. Each prisoner was allowed to write and receive mail. Russell wrote to his family and let them know that he was a prisoner of war and that he was okay. He also wrote to his girlfriend, Imogene.

The prisoners also used their creative abilities. Prisoners painted pictures made from anything they could get their hands on. Some of the paintings were on paper and some were painted on the walls. They even made up their own Christmas cards during the second Christmas in the camp.

Christmas passed and day by day the men endured the hardships as prisoners of war. Then, in April 1945, Russell and the other prisoners who dreamed of the day the war would end begin to realize that their dream was about to become a reality. The Russian front was moving closer. The guns could be heard at night. They got closer and closer each day and then one morning the prisoners were called into formation. The Nazis told them, "We are leaving the camp."

The March, April 8, 1945–April 26, 1945

On April 8, 1945, 4,000 of the prisoners began an 18-day march. The march covered 281 miles and ended at Braunau, Austria. The marching was divided into eight groups of 500 men with an American leader in charge of each group, guarded by 20 Nazi guards and two German police dogs. They averaged 20 kilometers each day and at night they stayed in barns, open fields, and alongside roads regardless of the weather conditions.

Russell recalls the march: "They moved us out of the camp on April 8, 1945, because the Russians were moving in. We walked 281 miles in 19 days. We went through a little town called Braunau, Austria, which is Hitler's birthplace. During the march we saw hundreds of Jews marching the opposite way we were going. If they fell out of line, the Germans just shot them like cattle. I saw them shoot several of them. The Americans didn't drop out. We had groups of five hundred and if someone got in trouble everyone else stepped in and helped. We had American planes coming over dropping leaflets telling us who they were and to stay together and not to try to escape because they were going to get us. We walked from daylight till dusk. We just stayed in the field or on the side of the road at night. We went across some mountains and we were higher than the clouds on one of them during the march. We reached Braunau after 18 days and we couldn't move any further because we were sandwiched between the Americans to our front and the Russians, who were coming up to our rear. The Germans took us into a nearby woods and left us."

Liberation, May 4, 1945

"Across the river [General George S.] Patton's 3rd Army was set up. We were sandwiched between them and the Russians so the Germans put us in some big woods and left. The next day, on May 4th, Patton's units came across the river and found us. When Patton's Army came through they were moving fast. They dropped guns and ammunition and told us to take care of ourselves. They left a couple of officers in charge of us and left. We were there about three days and we roamed the countryside looking for food. Three days later they moved us to an airfield and put us on C-47s. We flew to Camp Lucky Strike in France. We were there for about three weeks. We were given medical treatment, new clothes, and plenty of food. I was fortunate compared to many of the prisoners because I only suffered from some frostbite to my hands and my weight loss was about ten pounds. Many of the prisoners never made it back and many of those that did suffered much worse than I did."

Homeward Bound, June 12, 1945

On June 12 Russell boarded the USS *All American* bound for the United States. Russell set foot on American soil a couple of weeks later and headed for home on a thirty day leave. After reminiscing with his family, he headed to his girlfriend Imogene's house. They spent much of his leave together and then after thirty days he received a letter from the Army. "I was to report to Florida for recuperation. The letter stated that if you are going to bring your wife you better let us know. I wasn't even married. I told Imogene that if we were going to get married we better do it now because the government was going to pay for our way to Florida. We got married and went to Florida. A few weeks later I went to Chicago and was discharged on September 24, 1945."

POINT OF INTEREST

Hogan's Heroes

During the 1960s the television series *Hogan's Heroes* hit the air. The hit comedy series portrayed prisoners of war in Nazi prison camp. The setting was based on Stalag XVIIB.

Appendix A. Japanese Prisoner of War Camps, 1941–1945

CAC or CIC (Civilian) and POW (Military) Prison Camps

Philippine Islands

Manila Area

Assumption Convent
Atenco De Manila
Bachrach Garage
Bilibid
Camp Murphy
Christ the King Seminary
Doctors Hospital
Ft. Mckinley
Ft. Santiago
Engineer Island
Holy Ghost Children's Home
Hospico de San Jose
Las Pinas (at Paranaque)
Malate Church
Mary Chiles Hospital
National Psychopathic Hospital
Nichols Field
Nielson Field
Paranaque
Philippine T.B. Hospital
Port Terminal Bldg.
Remedio's Hospital
San Lazaro Hospital
Santa Catalina Hospital
St. Joseph's Hospital
St. Luke's Hospital
Santiago Hospital
Santo Tomas University
Sternberg General Hospital
Sulphur Springs Hotel
Zablan Field
Luzon Island Other Than Manila:

Baguio

Baguio Hospital
Brent School
Camp John Hay
Camp Holmes
Bayambang
Bilibid, New, at Mutinlupa

Cabanatuan

Cabanatuan No. 1
Cabanatuan No. 2
Cabanatuan No. 3
Clark Field
Limay, Bataan
Lipa, Batangas
Los Banos
Nasugu
O'Donald

Paracale
Pasay
POW Camp No. 17
San Juan Camp
Tagaytay
Tarlac
Tayabas
Tuy A.F.B.

Other Islands in the Philippines

Bohol I.
Tagbilaran

Caballo I.
Ft. Hughes

Cebu
Cebu City

Corregidor
Ft. Mills (Camp No. 7)
Malinta Tunnel Hospital
Ninety-second Garage

Coyu I.

El Fraile I.
Ft. Drum

Leyte I.
Tacloban

Manamoc I.
Davao Penal Colony (DAPECOL)
Davao Port Area
Lasang
Malabalay
Matina Airfield
Sasa Airfield
Zamboanga

Negros I.
Bacolod

Pawawan
Puerto Princessa

Panay
Lloilo City

Samal I.
Santa Mesa

Guam Island

Agana

Wake Island

Indonesian Islands of the Pacific

Ambon
Camp Benteng
Galala
Laha
Liang
Tentoey (Tantoei)
Victoria Barracks, Ambon Town
Town Gaol

Borneo
Balikpapan
Jesselton
Kuching, Sarawak
Pontinak
Sandakan

Celebes
Makassar City

Menado Gaol (Military Prison)
Menado Military Barracks
Pare Pare
Poso
Rapang

Lesser Sundra Islands

Ampenan, Lombok I.
Foelie
Makoronen
Maumere
Oesapa Besar

Timor I.

Atamboea
Dilli

Mollucas: Haroekoe I.

Haroekoe
Pelauw

New Britain I.

Bita Paka
Kokupo
Rabaul

New Guinea

Manokwari
Prafi River Camp
Windehsi
Wiringgi

New Ireland

Kavieng

Sumatra

Bangkal Pinang (Banka)
Djambi
Galang
Kebondoerian — Camp 4
Koetatjane
Loeboekrama

Medan

Belewan, Medan Harbor
Medan Old City Guard Bldg.
Medan Roman Catholic Church
Poeloe Brajan
Padang
Palembang
Pakanbaroe
Pakoe
Rantauparpat
Sikarakara
Soengel Kariau
Talang Semoet (near Palembang)
Tandjoeng Balai

Java

Bandung (Bandoeeng)

Artillery Barracks
Bandoeng (Tjimahi)
Exhibition Building
XV Inf. Bn. Barracks
First Depot Bn.
134th Depot Bn.
Soeka Miskin Prison

Bandoeng Area
Civilian Camps

Ambarawa
Bantjeu Gaol
Karees Camp
Mageland
Moentilan
Semarang
Sindanglaja
Soerakaboem
Tjhapit Camp
Cheribon (Tjirebon)

Djakarta (Batavia) Camps

Adek Building
Batavia Bicycle Camp
Buitenzorg

Depok
Diaroza Hospital
Glodok Prison
Struswyk Prison
10th Bn. Barracks

Djakarta Civilian Camps

Boekit Doeri Prison
Galoekan
Gang Kanario
Gen Hauber
Kramat Rd.
Matramin Rd.
Meester Cornelius
East of Meester Cornelius
Ngawi
Petodjo Area
Soerakarta (Surakarta)
Struiswijk Prison
Tangerang
Tenah Abang
Tjipinang Gaol
Ziekensorg Hospital

Djokjakarta

Ft. Vredenburg
Lelos
Malang
Poerwekerto
Serang City Jail
Serang Movie Theater
Soekaboemi (Sukabumi)

Suburaya POW Camp

Darmo Barracks
Grissee (Gresik)
Jaarmarket
St. Vincent's Hospital

Surubaya Area Civilian Camps

Banjoewangi

Blambangan
Kesilar
Malino
Pamekssan
Tegalsanggar

Tandjong

Tandjong Priok (Kampong Kodja)
Tandjong Priork
Tandjong Police Barracks
Other camps named:
Camp C
Camp D
Camp X
Camp Y

S.E. Asia Mainland

Singapore

Alexandra Barracks
Batutiga
Bidaderi Camp
Blakenmat
Bukit Is.
Buller Camp
Changi Barracks
Changi Prison
Changi Seletar
Chinese School, Katong Rd.
His Majesty's Central Prison
Holland Village
Krangi Hospital
McPherson Road Camp
Nee Soon
Old Race Course
Orchard Road
Palau Brani Island
Palau Damar Laut (Jeep Island)
Paulau Blakang Miti
Pasir Panjang
Revalvary

Seletar Airfield and Naval Base
Sime Road Camp
Syonon Changi
Tanglin
Tengah
Thompson Road
Tyersall Park
Woodlands Road

Malaya

Alor Star (Kedah)
Ayer Hitam (Johore)
Batu Pahat (Johore)
Beng Nha Hang
Binton Is.
Endau (Johore)
Ipoh (Perak)
Jitra (Kadah)
Johore Bahru Hospital
Kluang (Johore)
Kluang non–I.N.A. Camp
Kota Braru
Kota Tinggi
Kualar Kangsar

Kuala Lumpur

"A" Camp, Military Barracks, Ipoh Rd.
"B" Camp (Western Camp)
"C" Camp (Chinese School near flour mills)
"D" Camp (Chinese School near flour mills)
Main Camp, Chinese School, Batu R.
Malacca
Muar (Johore)
Penang, Penang Is.
Port Swettenham (Selanger)
Seremban
Taiping Gaol (Perak Dist.)
Talok Paku
Yala

French Indochina

Saigon

Baria
Civil Jail
Nha Be
Polyclinque-Camp B
Saigon Docks, Jean Eudel St.
Warehouses 10 and 11
Tan Son Nhut Airfield
Baster
Battambang
Cholong
Haiphong Road Camp
Hanoi-Gialam Airport
Hanoi
Mytho
Phnom Penh
Savannaket
Tankin

India

Andaman I.

Port Blair Jail
142nd Field Hospital, Calcutta

Burma

Akyab Jail
Bhamo Jail
Kalewa-Mawlaik
Mandalay Jail and Fort
Maymyo Jail
Maynigo Jail
Merqui Jail

Moulmein

Moulmein Jail — Camp No. 3
Wegale Camp No. 5
Mytkyina

Rangoon

Chettiar School, Kambe
Judson College
Kempelai Jail
New Law Courts Jail
Rangoon Central Prison

Ross I.

Tavoy
Thanbyuzayat
Victoria Point
Ye

Burma-Thailand Railroad Work Camps (North to South by location on R.R.)

4K. Camp — Khandaw
8K. Camp (Dutch)
25K. Camp
26K. Camp (Australian)
30K. Camp — Retphaw (Retpu)
40K. Camp — Anankwin
55K. Camp (Hospital)
62K. Camp — Mezali
70K. Camp
75K. Camp — Milo
85K. Camp — Apalon
105K. Camp — Angenaung Tadein
108K. Camp (Dutch)
Payu Thonzu Tuang
(Burma–Thai Border–3 Pagodas Pass)
Ban Nuang Lu
Dhamayiew No. 2
Dhamayiew No. 3
Dha Khanum (Takanum-Tauchan)
Kui Youg
Lin Thin (Rin Tin)
Gai Zai Yok (Kinsao)

Zai Yok (Konu)
Sra Si Mum (Tampli)
Tah Takua (Nong Takay-Toncha So.)
Ban Wang Yai (Tarsao)
Ban Lum Sum
Chungkai (Chonkel-Chong Kwai)
Ban Ko Krang
Tha Ma Kham
Ban Tah Maken (Tamaken-Tamarkan-
    Tamarkam)
Ban Nua
Kanburi Bae Hospital
Kanchanaburi
Ban Khao Pun (Cugkai-Khao Chong
    Kwai)
Ban Tai (Ban Dai)
Koh Samrong
Ban Kao
Wangkanai (Tonsamrong-Talat Tah
    Muang-Tamuang)
Non Tha Buri (Nondhaburi)
Nakhon Pathom
Wampo: 8K. (From Kanburi-double
    camp on both sides of river)
Bang Pong, North Camp
Bang Pong, South Camp
Ban Pong Hospital
Ban Pong (or Thai) Camp K. 1 from
    Ban P
Plek Ret
Non Pla Duk (Nong Paydock-Hnoh-
    npladuk)
Ban Haui Pong
Tagloh (Ban Pong)
Ban Muang

Thailand Camps Not Located

Wat Krang
150K. — Kanty

193K. From Ban Pong
260K. From Ban Pong
Conta (or Kanyu)
Kinranjok
Kunnyok
Tanrizaya Niaru
Tamajo

Thailand

Bangkok

Don Muang Rd., near airfield
Klong Toj No. 1
Klong Taoi No. 2
National Stadium, Bangkok
Rifle Range, near airfield
Vajiravudh College (Royal Pages College) Civilian Group
Vajiravudh College POW Camp
Bawa Sane
Chieng Mai
Hindat
Nagorm Nayok (Prachinburi)
Nike
Pechaburi (Pentenburi)
Rataburi (Rajaburi), Muang
Songkia (Singora)
Sukotai-Mesoth Road
Trang
Ubon (Ubonrajthani)
Uttaradit
Yang Yohng
Northeast Asia Mainland

China

Canton: 14 small work camps, including:

Anton
Cheung Ping
Cheung Pang
Honam I.
Pekkai
Pokong
Shemeen I.

Hainan Island

Cheung Kong
Hachow (Aichow)
Hoihow
Paksha Kong (Patsho Camp or Patano)
Samal Naval Base
Shinhlushan
Tinduk Mine

Hong Kong

Argyle St. Military Camp
Bowen Rd. Military Camp
Kowloon Section, Military Camp
Lai Chi Kok
Ma Tau Chaung (Matachung, Kowloon)
North Point Camp
Rosemarie Hill Convent
Samshuipo (Shamshuipo) (Camp S-Kowloon)
Sham Shui Po (Camp N)
Stanley Camp (Military Internment Camp)
Stonecutters Island
Yaumati

Kankow (Hancow) Internment Camp

Nanking

Peking (Peiping)

British Embassy
Fengtai Camp
Likuany Kiso Monastery (Linkuangkiso-Christ the King Convent)
Pataowan Monastery

Tai-Ping-T'sang Monastery
Prison Camp No. 1407, Peking

Shanghai

Ash Camp
Bridge House Jail
Colombia Country Club
Civil A.C. Eastern Area
Chapel C.A.C.
Franciscan House
Haiphong Road Internment Camp Shanghai
Jessfield Road Police Station
Lin Cha Lu
Lincoln Avenue Camp
Naval POW Camp
Pootung
Sacred Heart Convent
Shanghai Power Station
Shanghai Water Works
Ta Hsi Lu (No. 65)
Ward Road Jail
Yu Yuen
Zikawei

Shanghai Area

Chin Hua
Civic Center
Hong Chi Salt Godown, Kinhua
Kiangsu Middle School
Kiangwan
Linghwa
P'u-T'o Shan I. (Chusan Archip.)
Chikiang
Tinghai I. (Vhusan Archip.) Tingaad
Woosung

Shantung Province

Chefoo, Temple Hill CIC
Tsingtao CIC
Weihsein
Swatow
Tientsin

Yangchow: Civilian Assembly Center
Kiangsu:
Camp A
Camp B
Camp C

Yunnan Province

Chaiotoukai
Huangsikan (Wanglike)
Lungling
Mangshih
Shangkiakai (Maglien)
Teng Chung

Manchuria

Mukden

Fushun CIC
Hoten (Temporary)
Hoten — Main Camp
Hoten Branch No. 1 — tannery
Hoten Branch No. 2 — textile factory
Hoten Branch No. 3 — steel and lumber mill
Hoten, North Camp — U.S. Consulate Bldg.
Mukden Club Internment Camp
Mukden Military Hospital
Peiling Internment Camp
Hoten Branch No. 4 — Cheng Chia Tun
Kobahhashi Dairen
Sian (Changchun–Hsinking–Seihan)
Ssupingkai Internment Camp (Shihel)

Korea

(Chosen)

Jinsen Divisional Camp

Keijo

Main Camp
Branch Camp No. 1

Dispatch Camp No. 1
Konan
Korea Divisional Camp
Koshuyu I.
Pusan (Fusan)
Rempo
Repho
Ryuzan
Seishin

(Taiwan)

Formosa

Heito Prison Camp No. 3
Ingrin
Karenko
Keelung
Kingaseki
Shirakawa-Kagi, Camp No. 4
Taichu — Camp No. 2
Taihoku — Camp No. 1
Taihoku — Camp No. 5–Muksaq
Taihoku — Camp No. 6
Takao Hospital Camp
Takao POW Camp
Toroku
Tosei

Japan

Hokkaido I.

Asahigawa
Bibai-Machi (Branch Camp No. 3)
Hakodate Main Camp
Hakodate Divisional Camp
Kamiso Sub-camp (Sub-camp No. 1)
Mitisuishi
Muroran Camp (Kamiso Machi Camp No. 73)
Otaru

Sapporo Penitentiary
Temiya Park Stadium
Tomakomai
Utashinia (Hakodate Branch Camp No. 2)
Utashinia (Divisional Camp of Hakodate No. 3)

Fukuoka-Kyushu Island Camps

Amami I. (Ryukyu Archipelago)

Aokuma, Camp No. 22
Arao
Beppu
Camp No. 11
Futase, Camp No. 7 (or 10)
Lizuka
Kashi, Camp No. 1 (Pine Tree Camp; also spelled Kashi)
Koyagi Shima
Kumamoto Barracks
Kurume

Moji

Moji Camp No. 4
Moji Hospital
Nacama Camp No. 4

Najasaki

Camp No. 2
Camp No. 14
Camp No. 24 Senryu
Nagasaki Camp — former Franciscan convent
Omuta, Camp No. 17
Sasebo Naval Base
Sub-camp No. 12
Tobata
Yawata, Camp No. 3
Honshu (Southern) Zentsuji, Fukuo

Ka Camps

Camp No. 23
Higashi-Misome, Zentsuji Sub-camp No. 10
Innoshima Island, Sub-camp No. 2
Kochi (Kochi Ken)
Kure
Mitsu, Branch Camp No. 5
Motoyama, Sub-camp No. 8
Mukojima Island, Sub-camp No. 1
Myoshi
Niihama, Branch Camp No. 2
Ohama, Sub-camp No. 9
Omine, Sub-camp No. 6 (Higp Ton-oura)
Onoda, Branch Camp No. 8
Onoda, Branch Camp No. 9
Shimonoseki
Tamano, Branch Camp No. 3
Ube, Sub-camp No. 7
Zentsuji Principal Camp
Zentsuji Sub-camp No. 3
Osaka-Kobe Group Camps:

Kobe

Futatabi, Hoyoga No. 1
Kobe (7 miles west on Kako River)
Ito Machi, CIC Sub-camp No. 11
Kawasaki Camp — Kobe
Kobe Divisional Camp
Kobe POW Camp No. 31
Kobe POW Hospital
Koshian Hotel
Pago Camp No. 2 — Eastern Lodge CIC
Pago Camp No. 3 — Butterfield Swire
Seaman's Club CIC, Camp No. 4
Suzurandai POW Camp

Osaka

Amagasaki Sub-camp
Minato-Ku
Osaka Central Market Company
Osaka No. 1 Headquarters Camp (Chikko)
Sakai Prison
Sakurajima Camp
Sakurajima Sub-camp, Ichioka School
Sumiyoshi-Ku
Umeda Bunsho

Osaka-Kobe Area

Nagoya

Aichi CIC
Nagoya Main Camp
Narumi, Nagoya Sub-camp No. 2
Nagoya Sub-camp No. 10
Aoshi
Akenobe, No. 6-B Divisional Camp
Funatsu
Furashi
Fuse
Gifu (Nagara Hotel)
Harima, Camp No. 29, Wakayama
Himeji
Kiro Hata Divisional Camp
Kamioka
Kyoto (Branches Hakata, Kaira and Choki)
Maibara
Maisure (Maitsuri, Maizuru)
Notogawa
Oeyama (Oyama)
Roku Roshi
Shingu
Tanagawa
Toyooka
Tsuruge, Divisional Camp
Wakayama
Yodagawa Bunsho
Yokkaichi
Yonago
Yura

Tokyo

Akasaka Area
Franciscan Monastery
Kagawa Christian Fellowship House
Mizonkuchi
Narashino Airport
Omori Main Camp
Sekiguchi at Koishikawaku
Shibaura
Shinagawa:
Main Camp
POW Hospital
Shinjuki, Camp No. 1
Sumidagawa
Sumirejo
Suziki Aio No Moto Factory
Takadanobaba Camp

Kawasaki

Kawasaki No. 1 Bunsho
Kawasaki Dispatch Camp No. 5
Kawasaki Sub-camp No. 2

Yokohama

Achi Yamakita
Kanagawa, Tokyo 2nd Div.
Kanagawa, Kenko
Negishi Race Course
Nogeyama Park
Ofuna Camp
Old City Hall
Park Central Camp
Park Central Stadium
Totsuka
Yacht Club Boathouse
Yokohama No. 5

North Honshu-Tokyo
Control Camps

Akita

Aomori
Ashikago
Atami
Chiba
Chuzenji
Fukushima
Furmaki
Futatsui City
Fuji
Hakone
Hanawa, Sendai No. 6
Hiraoka Sub-camp No. 3
Hayashi Village, Yokosuka Dist.
Hitachi Ibaragi–Ken Camp (D-12)
Hitachi Motoyama
Kamita Kozan, Sendai Camp No. 11
Kanazawa
Kita Cotygara, Mura
Kosaka
Matushima, Camp 2-D
Mito
Morioka
Murakami
Nooetsu Prison Camp (Niigata Ken)
Niigata Sub-camp No. 5
Odate
Ohashi
Sendai
Shimodate
Shimomago, Hitachi
Shizuoka
Toyama
Tsurumi Sub-camp No. 5
Uraga
Urawa International Camp (Saitama)
Utsunomiya
Wakasen
Yamakita
Yamashita Camp No. 1
Yuwake Prison Camp

APPENDIX B. LOCATIONS OF GERMAN PRISON CAMPS

The list below is of Nazi prison camps, hospitals, work camps, and their approximate locations. Allied prisoners of war were held in these camps throughout the duration of the war. The information about these camps and their locations came from the International Red Cross, from prisoners of war, and from Allied intelligence.

Stalag (Main Camp), Approximate Locations

STALAG IIA:	Neubrandenburg, Mecklenburg, Germany
STALAG IIB	Hammerstein
STALAG IIE	Mecklenburg
STALAG IIIA	Luckenwalde
STALAG IIIB	Fürstenburg
STALAG IIIC	Altdrewitz
STALAG IVA	Hohnstein
STALAG IVB	Mühlberg
STALAG IVC	Wistritz, Czechoslovakia
STALAG IVD	Saxony
STALAG IVD/2	Saxony
STALAG VA	Ludwigsburg
STALAG VB	Villingen
STALAG VC	Offenburg, Bavaria
STALAG VIC	Osnabrück, Bavaria
STALAG VIG	Bonn
STALAG VIIA	Moosburg
STALAG VIIB	Memmingen, Germany
STALAG VIIIA	Görlitz
STALAG VIIIB	Teschen, Poland
STALAG VIIIC	Sagan
STALAG IXB	Hessen-Nassau
STALAG IXC	Thuringia

STALAG XB	Hannover
STALAG XC	Nienburg
STALAG XIA	Saxony
STALAG XIB	Fallingbostel
STALAG XIIA	Limburg
STALAG XIID	Waldbreitbach, Bavaria
STALAG XIIF	Freinsheim, Bavaria
STALAG XIIIB	Weiden, Bavaria
STALAG XIIIC	Hammelburg, Bavaria
STALAG XIIID	Nürnberg, Bavaria
STALAG XVIIA	Kaisersteinbruch, Austria
STALAG XVIIB	Gneixendorf, Austria
STALAG XVIIIA	Wolfsberg, Austria
STALAG XVIIIC	Markt Pongau, Austria
STALAG XXA	Toruń, Poland
STALAG XXB	Marienburg, East Prussia
STALAG XXIA	Posen, Poland
STALAG 344	Lamsdorf
STALAG 357	Kopernikus, Poland
STALAG 383	Hohenfels, Bavaria
STALAG 398	Pupping, Austria
Work Camp 21	Blechhammer

Marine Camp and Oflag (Officers' Camp), Approximate Locations

MILAG-MARLAG	Tarmstedt, Hannover
IVC	Colditz
VIIB	Eichstätt, Bavaria
VIIIF	Brunswick
IX	Hessen-Nassau
IX A/Z	Rotenburg
XB	Westphalia
XIIIB	Hammelburg, Bavaria
XIIIC	Ebelsbach, Bavaria
XXIB	Alburgund, Poland

Luft (Airmen) Camp, Approximate Locations

LUFT I	Barth, Pomerania
LUFT III	Sagan

LUFT IV	Pomerania
LUFT VI	Heydekrug, East Prussia
LUFT VII	Bankau

Dulag (Transit Camp), Approximate Locations

DULAG IVA	Saxony
DULAG IVG	Leipzig
DULAG VB	Rottenmunster
DULAG VIC	Hannover
DULAG VIG	Gerresheim, Rhineland
DULAG VIJ	Düsseldorf, Rhineland
DULAG VIIA	Freising, Bavaria
DULAG IXB	Hessen-Nassau

Lazarett (Hospital), Approximate Locations

LAZ IXC(a)	Thuringia
LAZ IXC(b)	Meiningen
LAZ IXC(c)	Hildburghausen
LAZ XA	Schleswig
LAZ XB	Hannover
LAZ XIIID	Nürnberg
Marine LAZ	Cuxhaven, Hannover
Luftwaffen LAZ	Wismar

Appendix C: German Regulations Concerning Prisoners of War

The German prisoner of war regulations presented here constitute excerpts from documents of the Nazi regime. These documents were captured by the U.S. Army's Provost Marshal General's Office shortly after the war ended in Europe. The regulations were translated by the Liaison and Research Branch of the American Prisoners of War Information Bureau. The list of abbreviations and translations is also provided by the Liaison and Research Branch.

Abbreviations of German Military Terms

Abbreviations	Translation
Abw	Counter Intelligence
Ag.E.H.	Section for Replacement Training and Army Matters
AHA	General Army Office
Arb.Ndo.	Work detail
AWA	Section for General Armed Forces Matters
B.d.E.	Commander of the Replacement Training Army
Bkl.	Clothing
Ch.H.Ruest	Chief of Army Equipment
Dulag	Transit camp for prisoners of war
Gen.D.Pi.	General of the engineers
Gen.Qu.	Quartermaster General
Genst.D.H.	Army General Staff
GVF	Fit for garrison duty in the field
GVH	Fit for garrison duty in the interior
H.D.St.O.	Army disciplinary regulations
H.Dv.	Army service regulations

Abbreviations	Translation
H.P.A.	Army Personnel Office
HV	Army administration
H.V.Bl.	Army bulletin
In.Fest.	Inspectorate of Fortresses
Kriegsgef.	Prisoner of War Department
Kv.	Fit for war service
Oflag	Officers' prisoner of war camp
Ob.d.L.	Commander-in-Chief of the Air Force
O.K.H.	Army Supreme Command
O.K.M.	Navy Supreme Command
O.K.W.	Supreme Command of the Wehrmacht [Armed Forces]
P.A.	Personnel Office
P.U.	Mail censorship
R.d.L.	Reich Minister of Aviation
S.D.	Security service
S.S.	Elite guard of the National Socialist Party
Stalag	POW camp for enlisted men
VA	Army Administration Office
VO	Decree
Wam.	Guard detail
W.A.St.	Information Bureau of the Wehrmacht
W.F.St.	Armed Forces Operation Staff
W.Pr.	Wehrmacht Propaganda
W.V.	Army administration

Supreme Command of the Wehrmacht, Berlin-Schoeneber, 16 June 1941

I. Chief group.

1. *Prisoners of war of alien nationalities in enemy armies.*

Frequently recurring doubts in determining the nationality of alien prisoners of war are now definitely resolved in that the *uniform* is the determining outward factor in establishing the fact of the prisoner's belonging to the respective armed forces.

Accordingly, Polish prisoners of war captured in French uniforms will be considered *Frenchmen*, while Poles captured in *Polish* uniforms will be considered *Poles*.

2. *The title "camp officer" instead of "camp leader."*

The title "camp leader" is not accepted in any of the regulations. It is therefore no longer to be used, and is to be replaced by: "first camp officer" and "second camp officer."

3. *Reward for the recapture of escaped prisoners of war.*

The OKW has requested the German newspapers to publish the following:

In view of the increase in the number of escape attempts by prisoners of war commonly occurring in the spring, the military and police services will welcome the cooperation of the general public. Persons offering effective aid in apprehending escaped prisoners of war may be granted financial awards, applications for which must be directed to the respective prisoner of war camp.

The reward herewith provided for are to be paid out of Reich funds.... The reward of one individual shall not exceed 30 marks even when several prisoners of war are apprehended. The amount is fixed by the commander of prisoners of war having jurisdiction in the respective prisoner of war camps.

II. Group I.

4. *Personal contact of prisoners of war with women.*

Certain inquiries addressed to the OKW make it necessary to point out the following:

The prohibition of 10 Jan. 1940 applies only to association of prisoners of war with *German* women.

It is therefore not necessary to submit a detailed report in cases of illicit traffic of prisoners with women of foreign nationality, unless certain circumstances make it a penal offense (rape, intercourse with minors, etc.).

The question as to the prisoner's liability to disciplinary punishment is left to the discretion of the disciplinary superior officer. The inquiry of the Army District Command V of 29 April 1941 I 3330 is thereby settled.

5. *Questionnaires for French officers.*

The French Armistice Commission had some time ago requested, in connection with the reconstitution of the French army, that newly arrived French prisoner-of-war officers in all the camps fill out questionnaires. Since the work is now finished, the questionnaires need not be filled out any longer.

6. *Transfers to officers' camp IV C Colditz.*

Several officers' camps frequently transfer to officers' camp IV C prisoner-of-war officers who have not yet completed disciplinary sentences pending against them.

As the few guardhouse cells in officers' camp IV C are currently occupied by prisoner-of-war officers serving sentences imposed by the headquarters of the camp, the transfer of officers to officer's camp IV C may be undertaken only after they have completed their previously imposed disciplinary sentences.

7. *Jews in the French Army.*

A transfer of the Jews to special camps is not intended; *they must, however, be separated from the other prisoners of war* and, in case of enlisted men, must be assigned to work in closed groups outside the camp.

Jews are not to be specially marked.

8. *Punishment of prisoners of war by the suspension of mail service.*

Several cases have been recently reported where camp commandants have suspended prisoner of war mail service as a disciplinary measure.

Attention is called to Art. 36, sec. 1, of the Geneva Convention of 1929 prohibiting the stoppage or confiscation of incoming or outgoing mail of prisoners of war.

Article 57, sec. 2, merely provides that packages and money orders addressed to prisoners of war undergoing disciplinary punishment may be handed to them only after the completion of their sentence.

The decision as to whether mail is to be handed out to prisoners of war under a court sentence rests with the competent penal authorities....

Supreme Command of the Wehrmacht, Berlin-Schoeneberg, 23 July 1941

3. *English books for training in radio broadcasting to foreign lands. (Talk work).*

In camps occupied by British prisoners of war several copies of the books named below will probably be found in possession of the prisoners:

Field Service Regulations, vols. 1 & 2
Manual of Organization and Administration
Field Service Pocket Book
Infantry Training, vols. 1 & 2
Cavalry Training
Artillery Training
Infantry Section Training
Engineer Training

It is requested that one copy of these books be procured & forwarded *directly* to the OKW/W Pr (IV h i) Berlin W 35, Bendlerstr. 10.

Should other books of similar nature not mentioned above be found it is requested that one copy of these too, be forwarded.

No statement as to where the books are being sent is to be made to the prisoners of war....

14. *Questionnaires on cases of death of prisoners of war.*

In case of death of a prisoner of war, in addition to the report to the Information Bureau of the Wehrmacht, a special questionnaire must be *immediately* filled out and submitted to the German Red Cross, Berlin SW 61 Bluecherplatz 2, so that the relatives of the deceased can be notified without delay (OKW file 2 F 24.

62a. Kriegsgef. Vi No. 135/11 dated 7 Jan. 1941). *Direct* notification of the next of kin of the deceased is not permitted. *Double reports* are to be avoided. Should the prisoner of war die while in a hospital, the camp is to be informed of the date on which the questionnaire has been forwarded to the German Red Cross. *No* questionnaires are to be filled out in cases of death of *Russian* prisoners of war....

Supreme Command of the Wehrmacht, Berlin-Schoeneberg, 1 Sep 1941

4. *Religious functions at prisoner of war camps.*
In view of the general lack of interpreters, it will be sufficient for a specially selected, qualified guard to be present at divine services in which only the *Sacrifice of the Mass is performed and Communion is given,* in order to see to it that the minister does not add anything in the way of a special sermon....

11. *Guard personnel in officers' camps.*
Complaints have been repeatedly made that guards, who are entirely unfit for their task by reason of physical disabilities (club-foot, impaired hearing, marked near-sightedness, etc.) or low intelligence, are being used for the surveillance of prisoner-of-war officers.
For the sake of the prestige of the German Wehrmacht, officers' camps are to use only such personnel as are physically and mentally unobjectionable and who are thus not liable to produce an unfavorable impression on the prisoner-of-war officers. An appropriate exchange of personnel within the guard battalions is to be undertaken immediately....

Supreme Command of the Wehrmacht, Berlin-Schoeneberg, 8 Dec 1941

14. *Supplying camp canteens with rubber collars for Yugoslav prisoner-of-war officers.*
The firm "Rheinische Gummi & Celluloid Fabrick," Mannheim, was exporting before the war considerable quantities of rubber collars to Yugoslavia, for use by officers of the Yugoslav army. The firm still has on hand about 700 dozen collars, left from an order which could no longer be delivered and otherwise disposed of.
The Chamber of Industry & Commerce in Mannheim has approached the OKW with the request to be permitted to sell the collars to canteens of those camps where Yugoslav prisoner-of-war officers are interned.
Since the disposal of these collars, usable only by Yugoslav officers, is in the interest of our national economy, the prisoner of war camps in question are being informed of the opportunity to purchase rubber collars from the firm, Rheinische Gummi & Cellulois Fabrik Mannheim....

Supreme Command of the Wehrmacht, Prisoner of War Department, Berlin-Schoeneberg, 31 Dec 1941, Badenschestr. 51

7. Re: *Tin boxes of British fliers.*

British fliers brought down have been found to carry with them tin cans containing a small saw made of steel, a map of Northern France and of the North-German coast, chocolate, and concentrated food tablets. These tin cans presumably are to help the Britishers to avoid capture or to escape from imprisonment after capture. Such special equipment has been repeatedly found on British fliers. It apparently belongs to the "iron rations" (emergency kits) of the British air force.

Special attention is to be paid to this when capturing British fliers shot down or delivering them to a prisoner of war camp.

8. Re: *Informing newly arrived prisoners of war of camp regulations.*

There are cases on record where prisoners of war, newly arrived in a collecting camp *to be released*, and unfamiliar with the regulations of the new camp, were severely wounded or killed by warning shots or by deliberate fire.

Since the same regulations governing order & discipline in camps do not apply in all camps, care must be taken that newly arrived prisoners of war be immediately made familiar with the new regulations, even if their stay at the camp is to be temporary.

Posting alone on blackboards and in the halls is not sufficient.

A reliable prisoner-of-war noncommissioned officer or the camp spokesman may be entrusted with this task....

Supreme Command of the Wehrmacht, Chief of the Prisoner of War Department, Berlin-Schoeneberg, 11 March 1942, Badenschestr. 51

5. Re: *Marking of Jews*

The Jews in Germany are specially marked with a star, as a measure of the German government to identify them in the street, stores, etc. Jewish prisoners of war are *not* marked with a star, yet they have to be kept apart from the other prisoners of war as far as possible....

23. Re: *Cases of death of prisoners of war.*

Reports to the Information Bureau of the Wehrmacht on deaths of prisoners of war and the corresponding notices to the German Red Cross through questionnaires are to be drawn up in such a way as to obviate the necessity of further time-consuming inquiries.

The following is therefore to be observed:

1. The report of the death of a prisoner of war to the Information Bureau of the Wehrmacht must indicate the *cause* of death in exact accordance with the facts, and also give the *place* of death in a way to make the competent registrar's office easily identifiable. It is not enough, for instance, to state: "Shot." Rather must it be worded: "Shot while trying to escape," or "Shot in execution of sentence pronounced by ... division on..." It is likewise not enough to give as place of death merely "Camp Erlensbusch," but rather "Camp Erlensbusch near Village X. The exact location of a work detail in a death report is essential, even when such detail is located near a stalag, as it cannot be automatically assumed that the 2 places belong to the same registrar district.

2. The report on the death of a prisoner of war to the presidency of the German Red Cross constitutes the basis for the notification of the family of the deceased. The death notice is prepared by the German Red Cross and is transmitted to the next of kin through the local Red Cross office of the latter. *The questionnaire proper* is then forwarded by the German Red Cross to the International Red Cross in Geneva.

   In preparing the "death-notice questionnaire" the following is to be observed:

   a. The questionnaire must be speedily & fully filled out and promptly forwarded to the presidency of the German Red Cross, Berlin S W 61 Bluecherplatz 2. Only this agency is competent to receive such questionnaires. Sending same to any other agency is not permitted, even though the questionnaire was made up by the International Red Cross in Geneva.

   b. *Careful formulation of the cause of death* in case of unnatural death, as the questionnaire is to be sent abroad (International Red Cross).

   c. The nationality of the deceased must be given right after the name, and the name of the country after the address of his next of kin.

   d. The last question must be answered in the greatest detail, insofar as there are no objections to the answer becoming known abroad.

3. For the time being no questionnaire is to be filled out for deceased *Soviet prisoners of war.*

4. Deaths of prisoners of war are not to be reported to the Protecting Powers either by camp commandants, or by the spokesmen....

46. Re: *Poaching by prisoners of war.*

The Reich master of hunting reports a recent increase in cases of poaching by prisoners of war doing farm labor — particularly French.

Prisoners of war are to be told that violations of German laws are severely punished....

56. Re: *Polish soldiers belonging to the French Army.*

The nationality of a soldier is determined by the uniform he is wearing at the time of capture.

In doubtful cases, the place of residence of the prisoner of war before the war and the present residence of his next of kin will determine his nationality....

59. Re: *Engagements for work by British noncommissioned prisoner-of-war officers.*
British noncommissioned officers who signed a pledge to work but are no longer willing to do so are to be returned to the camp. Their unwillingness is not to be considered as a refusal to work. The employment of British noncommissioned officers has resulted in so many difficulties that the latter have by far outweighed the advantages. The danger of sabotage, too, has been considerably increased thereby....

75. Re: *Contact between French & Soviet prisoners of war.*
Soviet prisoners of war must be strictly kept apart from prisoners of other nationalities, particularly Frenchmen. They should also be permitted no opportunity for establishing such contacts at their place of work.
Strictest measures are to be taken against contractors who fail to comply with the above security requirements....

79. Re: *Position of prisoner-of-war officers with respect to German personnel.*
A particular incident has moved the Fuehrer to emphasize anew that, when considering the relationship between prisoner-of-war officers and German camp personnel, the most humble German national is deemed more important than the highest ranking subject of an enemy power....

81. Re: *Smoking by prisoners of war.*
Complaints are voiced by the Reich conservator of forests that prisoners of war smoke in the forests and thereby increase the danger of forest fires.
Reference is made to sec. 15 of the Compilation of Orders No. 5, dated 10 Oct. 1941. Attention of the prisoners of war is to be particularly called to the fact that smoking in forests is forbidden and that any infringement will be severely punished under German law....

85. Re: *Beards of prisoners of war.*
Prisoners of war wearing beards for religious reasons, e.g., Indians & orthodox clergymen, may continue to do so. Individuals enjoying a nonprisoner status, such as medical officers, army chaplains, and medical corps personnel may also keep their beards, if any....

109. Re: *Subjecting enemy prisoners of war to the operation of the Military Penal Code.*
The order of 10 Jan. 1940 forbidding association with German women and girls is to be made known also to French medical corps personnel taking the place of, or about to take the place of, the former medical personnel by way of exchange....

110. Re: *Handling of medicines.*
The provision contained in section 22 of the Compilation of Orders No. 5 con-

cerning the handling of medicines sent in packages to prisoners of war is hereby canceled.

The order *OKW 2 f 24, 82 u Kriegsgef. Allg. (A) Ab W III (Kgf.)* remains in force. The latter provides that packages found to contain medicines, restoratives, etc., are to be confiscated and their contents disposed of in accordance with section 3 of the order. Medicines, etc., are to be destroyed.

111. Re: *Prisoners of war as blood donors.*

"For reasons of race hygiene, prisoners of war are not acceptable as blood donors for members of the German community, since the possibility of a prisoner of war of Jewish origin being used as a donor cannot be excluded with certainty."...

114. Re: *Killing & severe wounding of British prisoners of war or civilian internees.*

Every case of the killing and the severe wounding of a British prisoner of war or civilian internee must be reported immediately.

An investigation is to be initiated by a judicial officer or an otherwise qualified officer. Where comrades of the prisoner of war or the civilian internee were witnesses to the incident, they, too, must be heard.

The result of the investigation and the minutes of the depositions are to be forwarded to the IKW/Kriegsgef. Allg. for notification of the Protecting Power....

167. Re: *Poison in possession of prisoners or war.*

Narcotic poisons such as "Kif," "Takrouri," & "Souffi," have frequently been found in parcels addressed to Arabian prisoners of war under the guise of tobacco packages.

These poisons are extremely harmful to health and are therefore forbidden in the French army. When searching parcels, particular attention is to be paid to these substances. They are neither to be delivered to the prisoners of war, nor to be kept by the guards. The packages are to be immediately destroyed....

171. Re: *Display of flags in prisoner of war quarters.*

Since the British government has forbidden the display of German flags in prisoner of war quarters, *British* flags are to be immediately withdrawn in all German camps. The prisoners are to be notified of the above reason during the roll call....

176. Re: *Reparation for willful destruction.*

Prisoners of war proved guilty of willfully destroying or damaging state or other property as, for instance, in connection with tunnel construction, are to be punished and, in addition, made liable for damages. Should the actual perpetrators not be discovered, and should the prisoners of war involved be British, the whole camp community may be collectively held responsible for damages — which is the customary practice in England & Canada (canteen funds)....

179. Re: *"Warning" wire: testing of wire enclosures in prisoner of war camps.*

Experience has shown that weeds growing within the stockade seriously obstruct the view of the enclosure. Several escapes in *day time* may be attributed to this fact.

Since the removal of the weeds is in most cases not feasible, a "warning" wire is to be strung within the camp — if this has not been done already — at least 2 meters away. The space between the warning wire and the main stockade is to be kept free of weeds.

Several escapes have recently been made possible by the fact that the wire fences, more than 3 years old in most camps, were damaged and rusted through.

These wire fences must be carefully inspected for reasons of security and existing defects corrected. Reconstruction or repairs should be proceeded with only within the limits of the available supplies of barbed wire. A new supply of barbed wire over and above the fixed quota is not to be reckoned with....

189. Re: *Treatment of Soviet prisoners of war refusing to work.*

Cases have been observed in some places where Soviet prisoners of war did not receive their prescribed food rations or received rations of inferior quality. This was due in part to shortages of supplies in some areas (e.g., potatoes), and in part to faculty organization in delivery of food (dinner at 8 p.m.).

The resulting drop in efficiency was frequently interpreted as a deliberate refusal to work and was punished accordingly.

Commandants are again directed to pay close attention to the feeding of Soviet prisoners of war and to remove any difficulties of local character. Should the contractor not be able to supply the prescribed food rations, the prisoners of war must be withdrawn to preserve for the Reich this valuable manpower before it has been rendered useless....

190. Re: *Withdrawal of boots and trousers from prisoners of war.*

The commanders of prisoners of war may direct within the military districts that boots & trousers of prisoners of war may be left with the latter for the night:

In large work details to save time;

In work details exposed to air raids;

For working noncommissioned officers.

191. Re: *Money rewards for recapture of escaped prisoners of war.*

Supplementing the reference order:

Rewards may also be paid for successful *prevention* of escape. The decision as to whether the action of a person not qualified to belong to the army, the police, or the frontier guard may be considered as having foiled an escape lies with the camp commandant....

199. Re: *Handling of tin cans for prisoners of war.*

In a few camps it has lately become common practice, when issuing tin cans to prisoners of war, to be satisfied with the opening of the can and a superficial examination of its contents, and then to hand the open can and contents to the prisoner. When underway, even unopened cans are issued as marching rations. It is again pointed out that, for reasons of security, only the *contents* of the tin can may be issued to the prisoner of war. Deviation from this rule may be permitted only in exceptional cases, as when other receptacles are not available. In such cases the tin cans themselves must be examined as a security measure prior to their issuance....

202. Re: *Sports events in prisoner of war camps.*

Since sports contests between prisoners of war of different nationalities have resulted in brawls, such contests are prohibited in the interest of good discipline....

223. Re: *Shooting & severe wounding of prisoners of war & civilian internees (except Poles, Serbs, and Soviet Russians).*

An inquiry by a court officer or any other qualified officer is to be initiated in each case of fatal shooting or wounding of a British, French, Belgian, or American prisoner of war or civilian internee. If comrades of the prisoner of war or civilian internee were witnesses of the incident, they, too, will be heard. The result of the inquiry and a copy of the examination proceedings are to be submitted immediately to the OKW Kriegsgef. Allg. (Ia), reference being made to the file number below. This report is to be designated as "Report on the use of arms by soldier X." A detailed report against soldier X will be necessary *only* when there is a suspicion of the latter having committed a legally punishable act and when an immediate court decision appears desirable....

224. Re: *Casualties of British, French, Belgian, and American prisoners of war resulting from enemy air raids.*

Deaths & injuries of British, French, Belgian, and American prisoners of war resulting from enemy air raids are to be reported in writing immediately after the raid to the OKW/Kriegsgef. Allg. (V), giving the file number below. The following are to be stated in the report:

1. First name and surname
2. Rank
3. Prisoner of war number
4. Date of birth
5. Wounded or dead
6. Address of next of kin.

In addition, the camp headquarters are to send carbon copies of the reports directly to: the Bureau Scapini, Berlin W 35 Standarten strasse 12 — when French prisoners of war are involved, and to the Belgian Prisoner of war committee, Berlin W 8, Hotel Adlon, Unter den Linden — when Belgian prisoners are involved.

A report is also to be submitted to the Information Bureau of the Wehrmacht.

The reports concerning special incidents to be submitted in accordance with the order OKW file 2 of 24. 83n Kriegsgef. Allg. (Ia) No. 71/42 of 17 Feb 1942, are not affected hereby....

228. Re: *Prohibition of the so-called "Dartboard Game."*

The so-called "dartboard game" is forbidden, as the darts needed for this game are to be considered as weapons and may be employed in acts of sabotage. The game is to be confiscated....

239. Re: *Transport of recaptured or unreliable prisoners of war.*

A certain case where a guard was murdered by 4 recaptured Soviet prisoners of war during transport after dark makes it appropriate to point out that recaptured prisoners of war or prisoners known to be unreliable should, as far as possible, not be transported *after nightfall.* Should the transport after dark be unavoidable, *at least*, 2 guards must be assigned to the detail.

240. Re: *Association of prisoners of war with German women.*

There are several cases on record where judicial prosecution and punishment of prisoners of war for association with German women was frustrated by the fact of their having been already punished disciplinarily, the matter being apparently considered as but a slight offense.

The camp commandants must apply the most rigid criterion in deciding whether the case is a mild one, as the association of prisoners of war with German women must be prevented at all costs....

243. Re: *Consumption of electricity by prisoners of war.*

In order to assure the most economical consumption of electricity, all lighting installations in the prisoner of war quarters are to be examined again; all superfluous lights are to be eliminated.

Lighting installations are allowed, where necessary, within the limits of the quota of Wm. Verw. V., part II, appendix 14, same as for squad rooms in barracks.

The following are thus allowed in officers' quarters:

     In rooms occupied by 1 to 4 men . . . . . 40 watts
     In rooms occupied by 5 to 8 men . . . . . 75 . . "
     For every additional man . . . . 10 . . "

Quarters of noncommissioned prisoner-of-war officers and men are allowed ½ of this quota.

For the use of electric utensils for cooking gift food, etc., written permission of the camp headquarters in each individual case is necessary....

246. Re: *Securing prisoner of war camps against escape attempts.*

    1. *Fencing in of the camp.* The wire entanglements between the inner and outer fences must be so concentrated that an escaping prisoner of war will be able neither to climb over them, nor to crawl under them. Anchor posts should be just only slightly out of the ground.

    2. The foreground of the stockade, as well as the space between the warning wire and the fence must present an open field of view and of fire. It is therefore to be kept free of brushwood and all other objects impeding vision.

    3. *Watch towers.* There are no generally applicable detailed instructions for the

construction of watchtowers. It depends on the topographic and climatic conditions of the camp and must provide the best possible field of view and of fire.

The functional shape of the watchtower is to be determined by the camp commandant....

252. Re: *Repair of private apparel of prisoners of war.*
Prisoners of war are permitted to repair their private apparel (including shoes) with materials from collective gift shipments. Such repairs are to be made primarily by the prisoners of war themselves. In case they are not able to do so, the repair job may be performed in the camp repair shops....

259. Re: *Supervision of enemy army chaplains and of prisoner of war chaplains.*
1. Enemy army chaplains and prisoner-of-war chaplains have repeatedly abused the permission to minister to the spiritual needs of the prisoners of war by creating unrest among the latter through inflammatory speeches.

    All chaplains are to be advised that they must, in their contacts with prisoners of war, refrain from exercising over them any inciting influence. They must be given emphatic warning and their activity must be strictly supervised.

    Chaplains engaged in inciting prisoners of war are to be denied the right to perform their pastoral functions and are to be called to strict account; the military district is to be notified of the matter simultaneously.

    In critical times visits to several work details by one chaplain (traveling preacher) will be forbidden on short notice and for a limited period.
2. Attention is again called to the reference orders stipulating that *sermons* may not be preached by field chaplains and by prisoner-of-war chaplains except in the *presence* of an *interpreter.*
3. In the event the divine service for a work detail can be held neither in the quarters nor in the open, it is the task of the stalag to provide a suitable room. The contractor may request, but not demand, that such a room be placed at disposal of the prisoners of war....

271. Re: *Raising rabbits in prisoner of war camps.*
In the future, the raising of rabbits in prisoner of war camps will be governed by the provisions of reference order 2 above. The OKW decree—file 2 f 24. 20 Kriegegef. (II) NO. 1261/49 is canceled.

The cost of raising rabbits will henceforth be charged in *all* the camps to the Reich. Angora rabbits, warrens, tools, etc., till now maintained with canteen funds, are to be taken over by the Reich at a price fixed by an agricultural expert of the Military District Administration. The proceeds of the transaction are to be turned over to the prisoner-of-war canteen.

272. Re: *Procuring wrapping paper for Soviet corpses.*
The camp headquarters will henceforth report the amount of oil paper, tar paper, and asphalt paper needed for the burial of dead Soviet prisoners of war

directly to the nearest paper wholesaler. The latter will then apply to the competent Army Raw Material Board for an army paper ration certificate. The further procedure is familiar to the wholesalers.

In view of the scarcity of the above kinds of paper, they may be used only for wrapping corpses. Their use is to be held to the barest minimum....

278. Re: *Internment of fallen or deceased members of the enemy armed forces.*

To remove any doubt as to whether prisoners of war shot during flight or in acts of insubordination are entitled to burial with military honors, the following is ordered:

 I. As a matter of principle, every honorable fallen enemy is to be buried with military honors.

 II. Flight is not dishonorable, unless dishonorable acts were committed during such flight.

 III. Cases of insubordination must be individually examined as to whether acts reflecting on the soldier's honor have been committed. Where such violations of the soldier's code of honor have been established without question, military honors during burial are to be excluded.

279. Re: *Accepting bribes by guards.*

A private first class on guard duty in a certain camp has on several occasions accepted bribes of cigarettes and chocolate from prisoners of war and permitted them to escape without interference, instead of reporting them to his superior at their very first suggestion. He was sentenced to death for dereliction of guard duty, for willfully releasing prisoners of war, and for accepting bribes.

All guard personnel entrusted with the custody of prisoners of war are to be informed of the above with the appropriate comments. The announcement is to be repeated at least every 3 months....

307. Re: *British prisoners of war.*

The instructions contained in the OKW memorandum: "The German soldier as prisoner of war custodian" outlining the duties of German guard personnel assume a particular importance with reference to British prisoners of war, whose frequent display of arrogance toward guards & civilians is not in keeping with the discretion expected of a prisoner of war.

The guards are to be instructed to severely repress any attempt of British prisoners of war to evade their full work duty or to associate with civilians beyond the limits set by the circumstances of their employment.

Only British noncommissioned officers who exert a beneficial influence on their British subordinates may be used in supervisory capacities. British noncommissioned officers found unsuitable for this task are to be replaced. Unless they volunteer for a job, they are to be transferred to Stalag 383, Hohenfels....

313. Re: *Death sentence of a prisoner of war guard member of a regional defense unit.*

The private first class Jungmichel, assigned to a guard detail at an officers' prisoner of war camp, entered into personal relations with a Polish officer interned at that camp. He supplied the officer, at the latter's request, with various tools, maps, and other items intended to facilitate the escape of this and other prisoners of war. Jungmichel was sentenced to death by the Reich court-martial for war treason. The sentence carried out on 5 March 1943.

The above sentence is to be made known to all the members of the administration headquarters and the guard units....

324. Re: *Use of identification tags by prisoners of war.*

To prepare and to conceal escapes, more and more prisoners of war use the device of exchanging identification tags with other prisoners, or of getting rid of them altogether. Such practices are to be prevented by the imposition of heavy penalties, if necessary. When calling the roll, a check of the identification tags must not be neglected.

325. Re: *Prevention of escapes through the gate in officers' camps.*

The entrances and exits in officers' camps — where this has not yet been done — must be shaped like sluices and provided with a double control. At least one of the 2 consecutive gates is to be occupied by a qualified noncommissioned officer, thoroughly trained for the task, from headquarters....

397. Re: *Taking winter clothing away from prisoners of war during summer months.*

No objections may be raised in the practice of leaving overcoats with prisoners of war, even in summer months, in areas subject to air raids — a practice designed to enable the prisoners to take these along to the air raid shelters during an alarm for protection against colds and to lessen the danger of the coats being destroyed by fire. For all other prisoners of war doing outside work and exposed to the inclemencies of the weather, the unit leaders are to decide on their own responsibility whether the overcoats are to be taken along to the place of work or are to remain in storage. The use of overcoats for additional blankets is forbidden....

404. Re: *Preventing escape by taking away trousers and boots.*

When establishing new work details, an appropriate room is to be set aside for the safe storage of trousers and boots taken from the prisoners of war for the night....

409. Re: *Transfer of prisoners of war.*

To reduce the number of escapes, prisoners of war scheduled for transfer to another stalag are to be notified as late as possible of such transfer, and not at all of their new place of internment....

421. Re: *Sale of cellophane envelopes & China ink in prisoner of war camp canteens.*

Effective immediately, the sale of cellophane envelopes and China ink to prisoners of war is forbidden, since these have been misused to prepare and carry out escapes....

422. Re: *Thefts from bomb-wrecked homes.*

When prisoners of war are assigned to wreckage-clearing jobs after air raids, their attention is again to be called to the death penalty as provided by the reference order....

429. Re: *Escape of prisoners of war in civilian clothes.*

Escapes of prisoners of war in civilian clothes are on the increase. Frequently civilian clothes are kept hidden in the barracks. The latter, therefore, as well as all other premises and spots accessible to the prisoners of war (corners under staircases, basements, attics) are to be constantly searched for such hidden articles. The contractors are to be urged to proceed in like manner in places accessible to prisoners of war during working hours....

431. Re: *Malingering by prisoners of war.*

Recent reports indicate that French prisoners of war frequently claim to suffer from stomach ulcers, the effect of which is produced by swallowing small balls of tinfoil showing under X-rays as black spots, similar to those produced by ulcers. The possibility of malingering must be kept in mind by the chief surgeons and camp physicians when prisoners of war are suspected of suffering from stomach ulcers....

462. Re: *Timely use of arms to prevent escapes of prisoners of war.*

In view of the increasing number of individual and mass escapes of prisoners of war, it is hereby again emphasized that guards will be subject to the severest disciplinary punishment or, when a detailed report is at hand, to court-martial, not only for contributing to the escape of prisoners of war through negligence, but also for failure to use their arms in time. The frequently observed hesitancy to make use of firearms must be suppressed by all means. Guard personnel must be instructed in this sense again and again. They must be imbued with the idea that it is better to fire too soon than too late....

504. Re: *Use of firearms against prisoners of war.*

The service regulations for prisoner of war affairs do not provide for any warning shots. Should the occasion for the use of firearms arise, they must be fired with the intent to hit....

513. Re: *U.S. prisoners of war in British uniforms.*

Prisoners of war of U.S. nationality captured as members of the Canadian armed forces are considered British prisoners of war, regardless of whether they joined the Canadian services before or after the entry of the U.S. into the war....

The uniform is the deciding factor....

517. Re: *Fuel*

To stretch the supply of fuel, experiments are to be made in the use of a mixture of coal dust (50%–75%) and clay, formed into egg-shaped bricks, for the heating of prisoner of war quarters wherever local conditions permit.

The result of the above experiments are to be reported by the military district administrations not later than *15 June 1944....*

522. Re: *Pay of American prisoner-of-war noncommissioned officers and enlisted personnel.*

The American authorities pay to all German prisoner-of-war noncommissioned officers and enlisted personnel an allowance of 3 dollars per month, regardless of whether they are employed or not.

As a reciprocity measure, all American prisoner-of-war noncommissioned officers and enlisted personnel are to receive, effective 1 Nov. 1943, 7.50 marks per month.

The American prisoner-of-war noncommissioned officers and enlisted personnel are to be notified of the above through their spokesmen....

534. Re: *Transport of prisoners of war in motor buses.*

In accordance with the existing regulations of the German Post Office Department, the transport of prisoners of war in motor buses is not permitted. No motorbus vouchers may thus be issued for prisoners of war, nor may the latter be allowed to use motor buses accompanied by guards.

In view of the special operating conditions of the motor buses, it is not possible to relax or cancel these regulations....

546. Re: *Enemy leaflets in possession of prisoners of war.*

Prisoners of war must immediately deliver to their military superiors (camp officers, leaders of work details, etc.) all leaflets, weapons, munitions, and other prohibited articles found by them after enemy air raids, or obtained in some other way.

This, together with the punishment to be expected for disobedience in more serious cases, is to be made known to all the prisoners of war....

565. Re: *Reports on British and American prisoners of war.*

For reasons of reciprocity, each capture of a British or American prisoner of war must be reported by the Supreme Command of the Wehrmacht *by telegram* to the respective enemy powers. The camp commandants are responsible for the immediate submission of a *written* report to the OKW/Chief Kriegsgef. Allg. V on all new British or American prisoners of war upon their arrival in the first stalag. Such report must contain the following data: Last & first name, rank, date and place of birth. The report to the Information Bureau of the Wehrmacht is not affected hereby....

572. Re: *Mail for British & American prisoner-of-war airmen.*

All incoming mail for British & American prisoner-of-war airmen is centrally examined in Stalag Luft 3, Sagan. The prisoners are to be instructed to indicate this camp only, under the heading "Sender," on all outgoing mail, so that the incoming mail is forwarded directly to Stalag Luft 3. A further examination of the mail in the individual prisoner of war camps is unnecessary.

209

573. Re: The prisoner of war camps must do everything within their power to prevent the rifling of gift shipments for prisoners of war, and to have such thefts uncovered immediately. Particular attention is to be paid to the shipment of gifts from camps to work details, carried out on the responsibility of the military services. Pilfering of gift shipments by the prisoners of war themselves is to be reported to the OKW....

576. Re: *British & American parachutists, airborne troops, & antiaircraft personnel.*

Parachutists, airborne troops, and antiaircraft units are constituent parts of the British & American armies. Prisoners of war from these troops' categories do not thus belong to the "prisoners of air force proper" in the sense of the "Provisions Concerning Prisoners of War" of 30 May 1943. They are therefore not quartered in the prisoner of war camps of the Luftwaffe but in those of the OKW.

They are put to work in accordance with the rules in force for prisoners of war of the respective nationality. However, paratroopers are to be assigned to work in closed groups and under special guard.

Since the above service branches within the German armed forces are parts of the Luftwaffe, the *questioning* of newly arrived prisoners of war for intelligence purposes is the task of the Luftwaffe.

Newly captured British & American parachutists, airborne troops, and members of air-defense units are therefore to be sent for interrogation to the "evaluation center," West Oberursel/Taunus, where only small units are involved (up to 20 prisoners). Where the number of such prisoners brought in at one time is 20 or more, arrangements are to be made in each case over the telephone as to whether the prisoners shall be taken for interrogation to Oberursel/Taunus, or whether the evaluation center West should send an interrogation detail to the spot.

At the end of the interrogation the respective prisoners of war are sent to the prisoner of war camps of the OKW....

583. Re: *Return of prisoners of war, recovered from illness, to their old place of work.*

Complaints are heard from management quarters about the slow return of prisoners of war from hospitals to their old place of work after recovery. The prisoners of war, again able to work, are kept too long in the camps after their release from the hospital.

It is the duty of the camp commandants to see to it that prisoners of war, released from hospitals as fully able to work, be sent back in the quickest possible way to their former places of work.

584. Re: *"Stepping out" by prisoners of war during work.*

Since the prisoners of war misuse the unauthorized "stepping out" for the purpose of escape or loafing, it may be recommended — as has already been done in some plants — that a fixed time be set for such practice. Exceptions are to be permitted only for reasons of health.

No generally binding rule is possible in view of the varying local conditions, the strength of the work details, etc. However, the stalags are to keep an eye on the problem, since uniformity, wherever possible, is greatly desirable as a means of avoiding the above-stated difficulties. Appropriate rules might be incorporated in the plant regulations applying to prisoners of war.

The stalags are to instruct the leaders of the larger work details to communicate with the plant managers in regard to the above matter....

589. Re: *Gate control of incoming and outgoing vehicles.*

Reports on escapes of prisoners of war indicate that the control of incoming and outgoing vehicles at the gates is not always carried out with the proper care. There are cases on record where prisoners of war have left the camps undisturbed, hidden under loads of sand, linen, etc. Care is to be taken that the vehicles are always closely scrutinized.

590. Re: *Quartering of mentally ill prisoners of war or internees.*

There is occasion to point out that prisoners of war or internees suffering from mental disorders but not requiring confinement in a closed institution must be kept in camps or hospitals in such a way as to avoid, under all circumstances, the possibility of mishaps (such as entering the area outside the warning wire without permission).

591. Re: *Organization of the Bureau Chef Kriegsgef.*

The Bureau Chef Kriegsgef. is organized as follows:

I. Chef Kriegsgef.:
Colonel Westhoff

Staff Group:	Central processing of all basic matters and
Major Baron V. Bothmer	of those affecting in common the divisions Kriegsgef. Allg. and Kriegsgef. Org., with the:
	a. Paymaster: Administration, salaried employees, and workmen.
	b. Registry.
II. Chef Kriegsgef. Allg.: Col. Dr. V. Reumont	General & political affairs of the prisoner of war set-up.
Group Allg. I: Lt. Col. Krafft	Treatment of prisoners of war and effects of the prisoner of war problem on national policies.
Group Allg. II: Major Roemer	The prisoner of war problem in its foreign-political aspects; escorting of representatives of the protecting powers, of the I.R.C., etc., on their visiting trips.
Group Allg. III: Major Clemens	German prisoners of war in enemy lands and members of the Wehrmacht interned in neutral countries.

Group Allg. IV: Oberstabsintendant Dr. Fuchs	Problems of administration of the prisoner of war set-up.
Group Allg. V: Captain Laaser	Welfare of prisoners of war in Germany, and mail & parcel service. Cooperation with German Red Cross & I.R.C.
Group Allg. VI: Captain Recksiek	Exchange, furloughs, & release of prisoners of war. Problems of minorities.
III. Chef Kriegsgef. Org.: Col. Diemer-Willroda	Organization of the prisoner of war set-up.
Group Org. I: Major Dr. Hausz	The functioning of the German prisoner of war bureaus and custodial forces. Distribution of prisoners of war (planning); statistics.
Group Org. II: Lt. Col. Reinacke	Officer personnel matters (commandeers of prisoners of war), prisoner of war-district commandants, camp commandants and their deputies.
Group Org. III: Col. Lossow	Labor service and transport.
Group IV: Maj. Elickhoff	Camp management, index-files of prisoners of war.

595. Re: *Individual requests for enemy clergymen for prisoner of war camps.*

Individual requests for enemy clergymen are to be submitted no more. Requests for enemy clergymen are to be collected and presented quarterly at a fixed date by the Military District Commands, as per model I and II contained in order OKW, file 2 f 24.

596. Re: *Spiritual care in army prisons.*

1. In accordance with the reference order, *no* religious services are to be held for prisoners of war in army prisons. Army chaplains, civilian and prisoner-of-war clergymen may render spiritual aid to a prisoner of war only when the latter is gravely ill or under death sentence.
2. The reference order is relaxed in that prisoners of war in military prisons may hold religious services among themselves provided they request it specifically in each case....

619. Re: *Securing of prisoner of war transports against escape.*

The freight cars for the transport of prisoners of war frequently carry boards in the sliding doors, arranged so as to pass in stove pipes. These boards are to be removed before shipping the prisoners of war, since they render the barbwiring of the doors difficult and can easily be forced.

To better secure the sliding doors of these freight cars, not only the bolts, but also the door casters may be wired....

640. Re: *Reward for capture of fugitive prisoners of war.*

The Reichsfuehrer and the Reichsminister of Interior have authorized the Criminal Police, in the decree of 14 Dec. 1943—S—V A 1 No. 978/43, to pay a reward of up to 100 marks for assistance in apprehending fugitive prisoners of war or other wanted persons. In case more than one person participated in the capture, the reward is to be divided proportionately. Should the amount of 100 marks not suffice to properly reward all the participants for their cooperation, the matter of increasing the amount is to be submitted for approval to the Reichsfuehrer and the Reichsminister of Interior.

Rewards for capture of fugitive prisoners of war are not to be paid anymore by the prisoner of war camps....

646. Re: *Confiscation of gifts from the American Red Cross bearing propaganda legends.*

Gifts of tobacco supplies have recently arrived from the American Red Cross bearing propaganda legends on the wrappings. Most characteristic are packages of cigarettes with the word "Freedom" printed thereon. These articles were confiscated on several occasions because of this legend. It has been found that smokes with these legends were sent to the prisoner of war camps with no malicious intent, but that it was a form of propaganda for American consumption only commonly used in America. Such articles with propaganda legends should not be confiscated, provided the legends are not of outspoken anti–German character and provided there was no malicious intent on the part of the sending agency. The tobacco articles are to be released upon removal of the wrapping. In case of doubt the OKW is to be consulted.

The American Red Cross has been notified and has promised to make sure that further gifts to prisoners of war are free of all propaganda; it has, however, requested that shipments already packed be accepted.

647. Re: *Handling of prisoner of war mail for American prisoners of war & civilian internees.*

Letters and parcels arriving from U.S.A. for American prisoners of war and civilian internees have in a number of cases not been released by the camps for distribution because the U.S. postmark stamps contained advertising matter. These stamps were placed on the prisoner of war mail for no special purpose; they are the same used in the postal service within the U.S.A. The U.S. government has promised henceforth to refrain from placing on prisoner-of-war mail any legends relating to the present war. Mail is therefore to be released for distribution provided the postmark stamps and other legends are not of an unspoken anti–German character and where no malicious intent is discernible....

677. Re: *Supplying prisoners of war with beer.*

The reference order is hereby modified to the effect that henceforth not more than five liters of beer may be released monthly for prisoners of war and military internees in prisoner of war camps (Polish and Soviet-Russian prisoners included)....

679. Re: *Fixing of bayonets while guarding prisoners of war.*

It is in order to call attention to sec. 475 of the Compilation of Orders 30 of 16 Oct. 1943, whereby guards are to stand with their rifles loaded and placed at "safe" and their bayonets fixed, unless the camp commandant, for special reasons, orders a deviation from that rule. This order is extended to provide that guard details accompanying prisoners of war on transports or on their way from and to work have their bayonets fixed. French bayonets, which are too long, can be ground down to the standard size of German bayonets....

685. Re: *Use of sidewalks by prisoners of war.*

It is in order to point out that prisoners of war conducted through cities by guard details, singly or in groups, are not permitted to use the sidewalks but must use the roadway, like the smallest troop unit on the march.

Prisoners of war from broken ranks of work commandos marching alone from and to work are permitted to use the sidewalks, but must, when same are crowded, step off into the roadway....

687. Re: *Private conversation between German soldiers and prisoners of war.*

All conversation between German soldiers and prisoners of war not justified by the needs of the service or the work assignment is forbidden.

It is the primary responsibility of the company commanders to educate their subordinates to the importance of maintaining the proper distance between themselves and the prisoners of war and to put a stop to all attempts of the prisoners to start unauthorized conversations....

692. Re: *Assault on guards.*

Lately several guards have been attacked and killed while transferring prisoners of war after dark.

Prisoners of war are to be moved on foot after dark only in case of utmost necessity, and only under particularly vigilant surveillance.

Attention is to be directed continually to this prohibition and to the danger of attack....

713. Re: *Instructing guard personnel in the guard regulations.*

There is reason to point out that guard personnel engaged in guarding prisoners of war must be given continuous instruction in guard regulations. It does not suffice to hand the guard personnel a copy of the regulations and expect them to study its contents by themselves.

714. Re: *Taking away boots and trousers from prisoners of war in work details.*

In order to render more difficult the escape of prisoners of war assigned to and quartered in work details, their boots and trousers are generally to be taken away for the night and stored in such a manner as to make their recovery by the prisoners impossible.

715. Re: *Air defense measures in the prisoner of war service.*

During an air raid alarm prisoners of war may be assigned to the defense of their own quarters and workshops in exactly the same manner as the German employees.

After the all-clear signal they may also be assigned to damage-control work in other places, but, in this case, must be kept under safe, regular surveillance.

716. Re: *Disposal of tin cans sent to prisoners of war.*

The regulations contained in the above reference, insofar as they concern the handling of tin cans sent to prisoners of war, are summarized, changed as follows:

1. Tin cans of all kinds, with or without their contents (from parcels received from home, from love gifts, from rations supplied by the army or the manager of the plant) may be left in the hands of individual prisoners of war in strictly limited quantities and under strict supervision.

Purpose of this regulation:

   a. To prevent the accumulation of larger amounts of food stuffs to facilitate escape.

   b. To eliminate empty tin cans as means of escape, such as in the construction of tunnels, the preparation of imitation buckles, etc.

   c. To prevent the smuggling of forbidden messages and of objects useful in escape, espionage, and sabotage.

2. The individual prisoner of war may be allowed a maximum of six tin cans for the storage of his food supplies (meat, spread on bread, sugar, tea, etc.), provided no other means of storage are available in sufficient quantities and provided there is no danger of the wrong use of these cans.

Before a filled tin can is issued, it must be examined before and after opening; such examination may be limited to random sampling in the case of tin cans (and tubes) sent by the British and American Red Cross in standard packages.

3. When new tin cans are issued, the old ones must be withdrawn.

Used tin cans must be emptied, cleaned, and stored in a place out of reach of the prisoners of war. They must be sent every three months to the scrap-metal recovery place, together with tin cans used by the German troops.

4. Compliance with regulations 1, 2, and 3 is to be enforced by orders of the camp commandants; these are to reach down to the smallest labor commandos....

718. Re: *Behavior of prisoners of war during air raids.*

  1. *Guarding of prisoner of war labor commandos.* In work shops which, accord-

ing to the air defense regulations, must be vacated by their crews during air raids, provisions must be made, in agreement with the shop management, that the prisoners of war be kept at all time under surveillance by the guards and latter's assistants while leaving the premises and remaining outside of same, as well as while returning thereto. Alarm plans are to be prepared fixing the place of the air raid shelters and the ways of reaching same.

2. *Marching prisoners of war seeking protection in public and private air raid shelters.*

No objection may be raised against prisoners of war on march seeking protection in public air raid shelters in a sudden air attack; private shelters, too, may be used by prisoners of war in an emergency, provided the number of the prisoners is small.

It is presumed that the German civilian population will take precedence and that the prisoners of war will be kept close together in one room or one place. Dispersal among the civilian population is forbidden. In case of need, the prisoners of war may be distributed under guard in smaller groups in several parts of the air raid shelter.

Details are to be fixed in agreement with the local air raid authorities....

729. Re: *Civilian clothing confiscated from individual packages sent to prisoners of war.*

Civilian clothes sent to prisoners of war by their next of kin are not to be placed in safekeeping, but must be confiscated. Relatives of prisoners of war well know that civilian clothes are not allowed to be sent to the latter. Confiscated civilian clothes are to be treated like clothes of recaptured escaped prisoners. Civilian clothes must not be sent to receiving camps for safekeeping when prisoners of war are transferred (also when they are delivered at army prisons)....

738. Re: *Air raid shelter trenches.*

In a number of cases prisoners of war have declared through their spokesman their unwillingness to work on air raid shelter trenches. Such a refusal on the part of a group of prisoners of war, in view of the internationally binding provisions of the Convention of 27 July 1929, is to be ignored.

The construction of temporary air raid trenches must therefore be continued without fail.

739. Re: *Use of confiscated gift packages.*

When gift packages of collective shipments are confiscated on the basis of the above order, or for some other compelling reason, the confiscated items are to be disposed of as follows:

1. Confiscated *articles of food* from gift packages are to be used in the preparation of meals in the kitchen; in that case the food rations supplied by the Reich may be correspondingly cut.
2. Confiscated articles of *consumption* like coffee, cocoa, tea, etc., are likewise

to be used in the community kitchen in the preparation of breakfast and supper.

3. Confiscated *soap* is to be used in laundries servicing prisoners of war, or to be given to prisoner-of-war hospitals for use in their respective laundries.

4. Confiscated *tobacco supplies* may be distributed as a reward for good work to prisoners of war of all nationalities, including Soviet-Russians. A receipt is to be issued and entered on the records of the respective camps.

Care must be taken that members of the German armed forces and other German nationals have no share in the confiscated gift packages, and that the assignment of the confiscated items for the sole use of the prisoners of war may be conclusively proved to the representatives of the Protecting Powers or the International Red Cross....

743. Re: *Working together of prisoners of war and concentration camp internees.*
The working together of prisoners of war and concentration camp internees has repeatedly led to difficulties and has unfavorably affected the efficiency of the prisoners of war. Employment of prisoners of war and of concentration camp internees of the same job at the same time is therefore forbidden. They may be employed in the same shop only when complete separation is assured....

745. Re: *Civilian clothes in prisoner of war barracks.*
Attention is again called to the regulation which forbids prisoners of war to have in their possession civilian articles of apparel, except properly marked work clothes. Such articles of apparel arriving in packages for prisoners of war are to be confiscated. Prisoners of war are allowed only pull-overs and underwear, insofar as the latter cannot be used as civilian apparel. Sport clothes, especially shorts, are to be handed out only after they had been specially marked as prisoner of war apparel. The way of so marking is left to the discretion of the camps. The prisoner-of-war quarters are to be checked again and again for civilian articles of clothing....

784. Re: *Ecclesiastical services for prisoners of war.*
Ref 1. Order OKW file 31 AWA/J (Ia) No. 2411/41 of 12 May 1941 paragraph IV.
  2. Order OKW file 2 f 24. 72 f Kriegsgef. Allg. (Ia) No. 10/44 of 10 Jan 1944, section 3.
In order to clear up certain doubts concerning the use of enemy clergymen in pastoral capacity at prisoner of war reserve hospitals, attention is called to the following:

1. In accordance with reference order 1, surplus prisoner of war clergymen — enlisted men or noncommissioned officers (i.e., members of enemy armed forces who were clergymen in civilian life and were captured as soldiers with arms in the hands) are to be assigned, as far as possible, to prisoner reserve hospitals as medical corps personnel. There they will perform their ecclesi-

astical duties in accordance with the provisions in sections 7 and 8 of this order.

[The next page has not been received from the archives, so the text will be picked up where it begins again.]

... allowed to perform their pastoral duties in:

stalags for enlisted men,

prisoner of war hospitals,

prisoner of war construction and labor battalions,

provided they assume these duties voluntarily.

b. The same applies to enemy field chaplains, provided they volunteer for service.

c. The use of these clergymen in accordance with 2a and b is contingent upon their steady residence at the place where they are employed....

810. Re: *Prohibition of the use of ink & colored pencils in letter writing by prisoners of war & military & civilian internees.*

Several cases are on record where prisoners of war have dyed their uniforms, blankets, and underwear with ink & colored pencils for the purpose of escape.

Ink & colored pencils in possession of prisoners of war and military and civilian internees are therefore to be confiscated immediately. Ink and colored pencils are no longer to be sold in camp canteens, and the issuance of same in all private shops for prisoners of war is to be prohibited.

Outgoing mail written with ink & colored pencils *before* this order was announced is to be forwarded. Such mail received for delivery *after* the announcement is to be destroyed.

Colored pencils may be acquired from time to time in the open market in limited quantities for drawing and instructional purposes; these are to be taken away every day after use and kept under lock and key. Strict control is necessary to avoid misuse....

812. Re: *Forbidding prisoners of war to produce glider models.*

Prisoners of war are for security reasons forbidden to produce models of gliders....

822. Re: *Working time of prisoners of war: here: on Sunday.*

As a matter of principle, prisoners of war are to work the same number of hours as the German workers on the same job. This principle applies also to Sunday work; it is to be noted, however, that prisoners of war, after three weeks' continuous work, must be given a continuous rest period of 24 hours which is not to fall on Sunday.

When a plant which normally works on Sunday is closed for that day, the right of the prisoners of war to a continuous period of rest is still to be respected. However, no objection can be raised to prisoners of war working beyond the usual working day and on free Sundays on *emergency jobs* when German workers or the German population are required to take part in such emergency projects.

However, the rest period thus lost on the emergency jobs must be made up for — even on a week day — if the last continuous rest period was taken at least three weeks back.

In special emergency cases prisoners of war may be called upon to work for the relief of same even when the services of German workers or the German population are not required. The decision in the matter lies in each individual case with the respective camp commandant, in agreement with the local authorities, the competent Labor Office and the agency in need of assistance....

837. Re: *Verification of personal data supplied by escaped and recaptured prisoners of war.*

Recaptured prisoners of war often falsely give to the camp authorities, to whom they have been delivered, names and identification numbers of other prisoners of war of their former camp and of the same nationality, known to them as having likewise escaped. Now and then they try to hide behind the name and the identification number of prisoners of war whose approximate description and circumstances of whose escape they had learned at the very time of their own escape. Such attempts at camouflage are made particularly by escaped and recaptured prisoners of war having a court suit pending against them at their former camp.

Security officers of prisoner of war camps are to verify in each case the personal data supplied by recaptured prisoners of war from other camps.

838. Re: *Death penalty for prisoners of war for illicit intercourse with German women.*

The Serbian prisoner of war Pvt. Pentalija Kabanica, identification number 104325YB, was sentenced to death by a court-martial for the military offense consisting of illicit traffic with a German woman, combined with rape. He had rendered defenseless the peasant woman in whose farm he was engaged as laborer, and then used her sexually.

The sentence was carried out on 14 Sep. 1944.

The sentence is to be made known in this version to all the prisoners of war....

840. Re: *Killings and serious injuries of prisoners of war and civilian internees (except Poles, Serbs, and Russians).*

The reference order has often not been observed, with the result that the OKW has had again and again to learn of cases of violent deaths of prisoners of war through the Ministry of Foreign Affairs or the Protecting Powers. This situation is unbearable in view of the reciprocity agreements with the enemy governments. The following additional orders are therefore announced herewith:

To 1. Every case of violent death or serious injury is to be promptly reported through channels to the OKW/Kriegsgef. Allg. (IIb) (for exception see 2). In cases involving the use of arms, written depositions of the participants and witnesses, including prisoners of war, are to be attached; action is to be taken by the camp commandant and the prisoner-of-war commander ("Kommandeur").

The name, camp, identification number, and home address of the prisoner of war involved must be given. Should a long search for these be necessary, a preliminary report is to be submitted at once, and the result of the search reported later.

Reports are also necessary, in addition to cases involving the use of arms, in cases of *accidents of all kinds*, of suicides, etc.; written depositions of witnesses will be mostly unnecessary here.

To 2. Losses due to enemy action are to be reported immediately to the OKW/Kriegsgef. Allg. (V) in the form prescribed by reference order to 2....

848. Re: *Rendering prisoner of war camps recognizable.*

Prisoner of war camps in the home war zone are not to be made recognizable for enemy air forces....

851. Re: *Transport of enemy fliers brought down, or prisoner of war officers.*

In view of the present state of transportation, especially in Western and Southwestern Germany, no more railway compartments may be ordered or used in the trains of the public railway system for the transport of enemy fliers brought down or prisoner-of-war officers to and from prisoner of war camps (also camps for interrogation and classification of prisoners of war). In agreement with the competent Transport Command headquarters ("Transport Kommandantur"), freight cars are to be requisitioned instead and attached, as far as possible, to passenger or fast freight trains; in order to economize on rolling stock in small transports, the number of prisoners of war on each trip must be correspondingly increased. In particularly urgent cases troop compartments may be used in EmW, DmW, and SF trains ("Eilzug mit Wehrmachtabteile"; "Durchgangszug mit Wehrmacht abteile"; "Schneller Frontzug")....

853. Re: *Prisoners of war mustered into Waffen SS (volunteer groups).*

Prisoners of war who have voluntarily reported for service in the Waffen SS have had their lives threatened by their fellow prisoners of war for their friendliness to Germany and their willingness to serve.

Representatives of the main SS office engaged in recruiting prisoners of war for the Waffen SS in the prisoner of war camps are to be reminded by the camp commandants that the security of these prisoners of war requires that steps be taken to have them speedily removed.

Should the enlisted prisoners of war not be able to take their physical examination at the SS, the representatives of the main SS Bureau must, when taking the prisoners away, report those turned back to the original camp in order that they may be assigned to another camp....

876. Re: *Treatment of Jewish prisoners of war.*

Ref 1. Compilation of Orders No. 1 of 16 June 1941, sec. 7.

2. Compilation of Orders No. 11 of 11 March 1942, sec. 5.

The combined above reference orders provide as follows:

1. The bringing together of Jewish prisoners of war in separate camps is not

intended; on the other hand, all Jewish prisoners of war are to be kept separated from the other prisoners of war in stalags and officers' camps, and — in the case of enlisted personnel — to be grouped in closed units for work outside the camp. Contact with the German population is to be avoided.

Special marking of the clothing of Jewish prisoners of war is not necessary.

2. In all other respects Jewish prisoners of war are to be treated like the other prisoners of war belonging to the respective armed forces (with respect to work duty, protected personnel, etc.).

3. Jewish prisoners of war who had lost their citizenship by Regulation 11 of the Reich Citizenship Law of 25 Nov 1941 (R.G.B.I. 1941 I p. 722), are to be buried — in case they die in captivity — without the usual military honors....

894. Re: *Reports on escapes of prisoners of war.*

Mass escapes, escapes of small groups, or single officers — from colonel upward — as well as of prominent personalities represent such a menace to security as to render the disciplinary handling of the matter in accordance with paragraph 16a K St Vo entirely inadequate, in view of the possible consequences of such escapes. Detailed reports must under all circumstances be submitted concerning the activity of the custodial agencies which made such serious flights possible — whether through dereliction of duty or through mere carelessness.

895. Re: *Strict house arrest and preliminary (investigation) arrest of prisoners of war, including prisoner of war officers.*

A concrete case makes it appropriate to point out the following regulations:

1. An increase in rations through delivery of food and other articles of consumption by all outsiders, including the International Red Cross, is absolutely forbidden.

2. Additional food and other articles of consumption may be obtained by prisoner-of-war officers only through purchase, contingent upon good behavior, and in moderate quantities. In each individual case the approval of the camp commandant is necessary.

3. Tobacco may be obtained in quantity within the general limits provided in the smoker's card, but only when the danger of fire or disturbance of discipline is absent.

Note to 1–3: Prisoners of war under preliminary arrest, in order to obtain additional items of food and of general consumption, must also secure the consent of the investigation officer (leader) or the state attorney....

897. Re: *Escapes during transport.*

There is reason to point out that prisoners of war during transport sometimes try to use the toilet for escape. The guards must therefore, as a rule, accompany the prisoner of war to the toilet on transports and must keep their eyes on him with the door open. Should the prisoner of war close the toilet door with the intention to escape, the guard must fire on him through the door without warning.

INDEX

Index